ReShape™: The Art Of SheAffirmatively™ Believing in Your Self:

A Womin-Affirmative™ SheChange™ Self-Workbook On ReShaping™ A SistahPeacefully™ WellBalanced™ Lifestyle

AfraShe Asungi, HHHAS, MFA, LCSW, ReShaper™

Maatfully ™ WellBalanced™ For Life Series
A subdivision of Mamaroots® Maasaum ™ Living Publishing House
~ An Independent Publisher.

IMPORTANT NOTE TO OUR READERS:

This book has been written and published for informational and educational purposes only. It is not intended to serve as medical advice or to be any form of medical treatment.

This book is not intended to diagnose or treat any medical condition and is not a substitute for a physician. This book is independently authored and published and no sponsorship or endorsement of this book by, and no affiliation with, any trademarked brands or other products mentioned within is claimed or suggested.

All trademarks that appear in this book belong to their respective owners and are used here for informational purposes only. The author and publisher encourage readers to patronize the quality brands mentioned in this book.

Cover and inside art images & design:
© 2021 AfraShe Asungi, HHHAS, MFA, LCSW. All rights reserved.
Detail: An Afrakan® ReShaping™ For 4 Wimmin™ Suite™.
© 2011-21 Asungi Productions.

The information presented in this book represents the views of the publisher as of the date of publication. The publisher reserves the rights to alter and update their opinions based on new conditions.

This report is for informational purposes only. All material in this book are intended for informational and educational purposes only. While every attempt has been made to provide information that is both accurate and effective, this information in no way constitutes medical or therapeutic advice.

lease seek the care of a physician or psychotherapist
egarding any medical or psychological concerns which you may have.

The author and publisher do not assume any responsibility or liability for damages of any kind resulting directly or indirectly from the implementation of information given in this book. Any use or application of the material in the following pages is at the reader's discretion and is the reader's sole responsibility.

First Printing: 2021

ISBN: 9798486263989

Publisher: Maatfully ™ WellBalanced™ For Life Series
A subdivision of Mamaroots® Maasaum™ Living Publishing House
~ An Independent Publisher.

Contact: www.Aparthamaat.com
Or: https://SheKulturalStudios.com

May you be Blessed to live Maatfully™ every day . . .

Honoring Our Selves & Our Glorious Mamaroots™
Through Maatful™ Practice, Remembrance, Praise, Imploration and Celebration . . .

TABLE OF CONTENTS

13

PART 3:
28 Weekly ReShapings™ 257

A MAATFUL™ DEDICATION

AjubaMa™ . . .
I sing You Heartfelt honey nectar Praises, and I paint for You
Rainbow Colored Words of Appreciative Gratitude
across the Horizons . . .
~ AfraShe Asungi

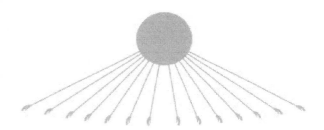

I respectfully write this text in loving memory and honor of each of my Unnamed, but deeply remembered—MeraatAbtep MatiMas AnSistahs™ of my TaNubian™ Blessed lineage of (Greatma) Ella Gilliam, (Grandmas) Mabel Wilson, Mamie Dwyer Moses, and (mama) Marian Sara Falami—as a talent of love, respect and reverent gratitude.

May You continue to Smile MaatSheConscience™ & WellBalance™ upon me. May Your ShephatiMaat™ Strength and SheDetermination™ live through me, as I earnestly continue to strive to pass on Our Timeless Knowledge and AfraShedoms™.

I Maatfully™ dedicate, pay homage and offer Endless Gratitude, to all AnSistahral™ SheForces™ Who Assist and Guide me on my earthly Journey . . . May You Continue to avail me of Maatful™ Love, Courage and Compassion to be UratHatMaKat™ AfraKamaati AfraSeshata™; enabling me to maintain the Afrawakened™ capacity to pass on Our Ageless Commission.

AjubaMa™! Great Makers of Rainbowed Wisdom and Golden SheMystery™; Ochun, Yemaya, Oyeye, SeshatiMa™, NathRa, Hathera, Basat, Nebhat, MaatiMa™, Sati

Hatepat, Metchat Natra. Maasa Nataraa™: Our 9 Mamas of Our Living Houses of Arts-Sciences . . . Who are Eternally a Source of SheInspiration™ . . . .

My deepest gratitude, respect and love to all my relations and my extended family of kin and friends. I will always cherish our friendships. Heartfelt Blessings of Ajuba™ Thanks and Homage to Our RootSistahs™ of Our Afrakan®/ AfraKamaati® Sistahood, MAMAROOTS®: Ajama-Jebi™ for all of your MaatSheConsciousness™ and AfraWominSpirited™ Being . . . that has been . . . and will ever be . . .

My heartfelt gratitude and myriad thanks to all who have walked before, besides and above me on this Lifeway Path of MaatiMa™. SaMaatiMa to my Immortal Thousand-Lotus-Petals Self for Maatful™ Knowing and Being—again and again . . . Ajuba gratitude to all those who have helped me to Maatfully™ Know Who I Really Am . . .

I Maatfully™ Dedicate, and offer my Heartfelt Blessing to my MatriSati™ daughter, Jajube ~ Bhudu Saatimiyansan, and to my maternal Meraabti™ nieces, Marian Dee

Dee and Autumn Crystal -- whom I now walk before, besides and above on this Lifeway Path of MaatiMa™ . . . Great AatNebti, AfraSheBaat™, May You Eternally Protect & Guide Your seeking daughters.

UM'Netesh Arat Ta Thaath, Mat Sekhemaat Hatchat Sankhat. Satineb Ajuba Ma . . .™

I Maatfully™ Dedicate, and offer my Heartfelt Thanks to Our clients and

Sistahs who have encouraged me that I really NEEDED TO create this ReShaping™ Self-Workbook . . . and so, after some 10 + years Dearest Sistahs, here it is . . .

 *Nehast Mas™ . . .*

Acknowledgments
Praises & Gratitude

What I wish best for my Self, I wish it for my friends too . . .
~ A Tuareg Proverb

here is just not enough room to properly thank everyone who has touched my GoodHeart™ and therefore, in some way have contributed to that which has become this text . . .

. . . Please Know that I am eternally grateful for your insightful opinions, guidance and supportive contribution over the years . . . know that while unnamed here, that I Maatfully™ carry each of you in my GoodHeart™ (from Whom, I am continually SheInspired™) to do BOTH the Inner and the Outer Work, as I Journey on this Ever-twisting Path of Maatful™ Knowing . . . I offer my appreciation and thanks to you all . . . Appreciative thanks to any and all of my own life teachers and mentors [formal or informal embodied or disembodied] for their Great Gifts of Insight. Maatful™ thanks to those, who like me, have dedicated their lives to earnest metaphysical study, and therefore left a body of work [scattered and sparse as it may be in some cases] for me to ponder. Thank you so much for coming into my SheConsciousness™.

I Dedicate, pay homage and offer Gratitude to all AnSistahral™ Guiding Forces Who Maatfully™ assist and join me on this absolutely SheInspired™ Journey . . .

My deepest Gratitude, respect and love to all my relations and my extended family of kin and friends. I cherish our relationships and friendships. Heartfelt Blessings of Ajuba Thanks and Praises to RootSistahs™ of Our Afrakan®/ AfraKamaati® Sistahood, MAMAROOTS®: Ajama-Jebi™ for all of your MaatSheConsciousness™ and AfraWomanSpirited™ Being . . . that has been . . . and will ever be . . . "the Wind beneath my Wings. . ."

23

Heartfelt Gratitude and thanks to all who've walked before, besides and above me on this Lifeway path of MaatiMa™. SaMaatiMa™ to my Immortal Thousand-Lotus-Petals Self for Knowing and Being—again and again . . . Ajuba Gratitude to all who have helped me to "Remember Who I Really Am".

AjubaMa™ to the Enlightened artists and scholars, who pointed out the Way of Self-Transformation my long journey from Colored to Afrakan® . . . among them; Augusta S., Barbara C., Elizabeth C.; Billie H., Dinah (Ruth) W. (my Goddess Mama), Sarah V. Nina S., Dionne W., Sylvia M., Alice C., Abbey L., Mariam M., Dianne R.; Zora H., Toni B., Toni M., Alice W., Octavia B.; Katherine D., Eartha K., Donyale L., June J. and so many more.

Ajuba to you who have shared, walked, marked and inspired my activist/ SheKultural™ / Psychotherapist Path; Phil M., Gloria W., Angela D., Ni'am A., Lloyd J., Handy L., John O., Makeda D., Isis H., and Colette P.

To those whom I have Righteously and fearlessly loved/ sometimes could not love enough/ will someday come to fearlessly and Righteously Love: NebHatept Meraati to Jill W. (4 the lovefire), Sylvia M. (4 Ochun and a Higher Love), Luisa P. (4 the mystic depth and the Reki), doris d. (4 the two-headedness), Toni J. (4 the passion poem/ love and affection), MaryAlice B. (4 the Libra loyal-heartness), ahdri z. (4 the dub/ step brownsun rhyme), and to every other dear HeartSistah™, who've not been named, but who have contributed an abundance of golden-heartedness, which has blessed, invigorated, nurtured and loved me into Being . . . I offer Ajuba/ Ase-O to Iya Oni Dina (Beatrice A.) who has Maatfully™ held the Space for me as I sought out and engaged in this radical process of my own Afrakan® ReBecoming . . . Ta Nebt . . . Nehast Mas!!!

To my Dearest AnuKaBrotahs™, Bunia S., Keith P., Randy W. and Handy L., there just aren't enough Words . . . My humble Gratitude and Unmeasurable appreciation to you, who [amazingly so] have continued to be there, "holding up the Sky" for me through the years: my Cherished HeartSistahs™; Luisa P., doris d., MaryAlice B. and ahdri m.

 *Nehast Mas™ . . .*

About Our SistahPeacefully™ WellBalanced™ Therapy Process

. . . Peace of Mind . . .

*"It doesn't mean being in a place
where there is no noise, trouble, or hard work.
It means being in the midst of those things
and STILL Being Calm in your Heart . . ."*
~ Unknown Author

**ur SistahPeace™ ReShaping™ WellBalance™
Counseling & Coaching Mission is:**
*To bring about Proactive SheChange™ & Transpersonal Growth by
ReRooting™ Wimmin™ & unconventional folk in fulfilling and
productive lives (ReShape™) ~ which dynamically engages their own Unique, and
Potent Insights, Dreams & Possibilities . . .*

*To encourage Self-paced advancement toward [re]establishing an authentic sense of
WellBalanced™ & SistahPeaceful™ Self-Regard ~ bringing about dynamic,
meaningful SheChange™ and ReShape™ an abiding sense of SheInspired™ Inner-*

25

Strength, & Self-Resilience into the lives of each and every one of our clients . . . so that they may live happy, SistahPeaceful™ and productive lives.

Putting Our Mission Statement Into A More Practical Framework

Now, please don't let the uniqueness of our Womin-Affirmative™ language be off-putting for you in any way, because we can assure you that the actual hands-on approaches are, in fact, pretty simple, straightforward, accessible and "doable." ~ a bit like the mindfulness approach, itself, which, when described seems to be a bit "dense" and daunting if you are new to it, but in time becomes really, really simple.

And if you've ever tried to learn another culture or new language style after the age of 11 or so, [like calligraphy or hip-hop lyrics or even texting, if you're new to them] then we're sure you can recall just how difficult it was for you initially ~ simply because you were so unfamiliar with the meanings and definitions of so much of what you initially read, heard or learned.

However, we're also sure that within a short time, words and context which had at first seemed bulky, dense and "difficult" to you eventually became simpler more facile as you came to be more and more familiar with them as you practiced over time.

And similarly, you'll also find that our uniquely ReShaped™ Womin-Affirmative™ language becomes simpler to navigate through with use. You'll come to discover how our unique use of such Womin-Affirmative™ language is specifically purposed to assist you in making real and manageable Womin-Affirmative™ SheChanges™ in your life.

While you are engaged in our eclectic and dynamic blend of counseling or coaching approaches ~ you'll also be encouraged to use language, and personal meaning that will assist you to incrementally uproot and adjust any deeply internalized Self-depreciating, anti-Womin™ patterns of beliefs or habits that are currently impeding your desired progress to living a happy, productive and SistahPeaceful™ life.

You'll also learn just how it is that such deeply internalized beliefs are frequently the underlying causes of any irresolvable or immutable blockages and self-sabotaging patterns which can often frustrate or thwart some clients, even as they work diligently toward realizing, maintaining or sustaining (ReShape™) a renewed sense of emotional, mental and physical wellbeing and inner-peace . . . and to live happy, productive and SistahPeaceful™ lives . . .

As do many eclectic & progressive spirituality based practitioners, we believe that everyone's Soul Purpose is to learn and evolve. And so life's issues, problems and challenges are the way our Soul Selves learns, grows and assists us to know who we really are ~ which is why we're here ~ to actualize Our Knowing Purpose.

The goal of our SistahPeace™ ReShaping™ WellBalance™ approach and our Womin-Affirmative™ approach is to help you to identify and resolve the underlying conflicts so that you will also become more aware of who you really are, and proactively learn to naturally honor your Authentic Soul Self as a way to live a more fulfilled and happy life.

Far-too often Self-denial and depreciation are two of the most pervasive patterns we see amongst Wimmin™, because we are held captive in an unnatural, disorded, unconscionable denial of our Authentic Soul Self.

What this often means is that our clients have become disconnected from essential and very important parts of our Selves; for example, our Thoughts, Feelings, instincts, power, intuition, voice, creativity, sexuality, dreams, passions, and/ or their bodily vitality.

As a result, we often experience a disheartened lack of Self-worth and therefore are unable to naturally accept, love and nurture ourselves. In order to heal and restore our innate peace of mind, we must reclaim and reconnect with these vitally important parts of ourselves.

Many Wimmin™ are seduced by a surrogate "mainstream" Kulture™ into believing that our worth depends upon how we look and how materially productive we are. It's all about the external world of "doing".

Eventually, we find our Selves "stuck", aimlessly running around in surrealistic "emotional circles", never actually realizing the much desired and sought after "rewards" ~ a sense of fulfillment and true love ~ which are promised, yet elusive prizes for our superimposing a superficial passageway deep into the external realm of "false realities".

Our Authentic Self vested by our Divine Soul Self becomes desperate for this cycle to end; the true voice inside us warns us that something is "just not right", and becomes an inner-voice that will no longer remain silenced or forgotten.

This essential awareness of being "significantly derailed" from being who we really are, [our Authentic Self] often surfaces as the disordered symptoms of anxiety, panic, anger, co-dependence, mistrust, dissatisfaction, despondence, depression, addiction and more.

*"If you are going down a road . . .
and don't like what's in front of you . . .
and look behind you . . .
and don't like what you see . . .
get off the road . . .create a new path . . ."
~ Maya Angelou*

How Do We Proactively ReShape™ Our Selves ?

When we learn how to slow down and just "BE"; when we learn to make time to listen to our Authentic Soul Self; when we learn to make time to acknowledge and process our innate feelings; when we learn to make nurturing and loving our Selves our real purpose and calling; then we come to discover and naturally be who we truly are.

Then, we learn to dare to naturally love our Selves without apology. Then we find a True Sense of [Self] fulfillment, which we'd previously sought in food, sex, drugs, status, approval, perfect bodies and perfect careers.

When our clients come to realize that our "westernized" pleasure-seeking and "escapist" Kulture™ is unhealthy for us in countless ways; so much so that just being born into it, induces personal dis-ease and imbalance.

When we come to see how Wimmin™ whose dispositions are often deemed to be "sweet", "sensitive", creative, intuitive, non-conformist, unconventional, etc., are unfortunately pre-disposed to readily internalizing Self-negating beliefs and Self-defeating patterns.

When our clients come to learn to effectively strip away the unwanted layers of Self-negation and Fear; we come to learn to affirm our own True Selves, our own True Voices, and we come to Proactively ReShape™ and live "on our own authentically holistic and Womin-Affirmative™ terms". . .

. . . We'll work with you . . .
. . . as you progressively resolve, minimize
and make peace with any difficulties,
crises, or distresses that have significantly
impeded or derailed you . . .

We affirm that we can also learn to effectively strengthen our "emotional immune system" by learning how to love, honor and nurture our Selves. We can teach you how to use our proactive, Womin-Affirmative™ approach in order to successfully do this.

We can teach you how to mindfully re-connect with your Authentic Self, so that you can feel more confident, more Self-loving, content and more fully alive.

We can teach you how to compassionately nurture and love your Authentic Self; how to overcome and make peace with internalized fear, overly-critical Self-judgment and

Self-loathing, through the use of a variety of eclectic and holistic Self-awareness and Womin-Affirmative™ techniques and approaches.

We can help you create a SistahPeacefully™ WellBalanced™ lifestyle that is more meaningful, Self-affirming, joyously fulfilling and plain ole fun . . .

 *Nehast Mas™ . . .*

A Note To Our Readers

May you be Blessed to live Maatfully™ every day . . .
~ AfraShe Asungi

The Roots of Our Language

Writing is not my first language, but the pictographic symbolic imagery script of Fine Art is. This sometimes makes for cumbersome concepts when attempting to outline this symbolism in the form of letter script writing, which is (for me anyway) a much more limited form of Thought representation.

My perceptive gifts are akin to those of the ancient Enlightened SheScribes™, early SheCreatresses™ of DivineShe™ energy made manifest in synchronistic imagery.

Reading this book may seem somewhat difficult for some, at first because of the language "concepts" which I've intentionally included, Knowing the power of Thought ReShaping™.

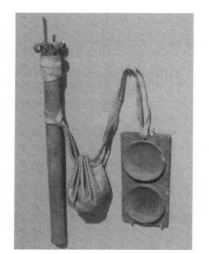

But I promise that, what was initially difficult for you will, in time, engender a unique perception and insight, as your day-to-day Way of seeing slowly shifts and realigns with (coincides with) Our unique Maatful™ SpiraKultural™ POV and Right Intent . . .

Our Use of Trademark Symbols

Understanding how this might be seen as cumbersome and capitalistic to some – it's

31

become a "necessary evil" in order to reduce deliberate misuse and misappropriation without any regard; and even to suppress Our divergent philosophy . . . by some, who are Afraphobik™, misogynous, or otherwise entrenched.

And to put an END to the intentional infringement (by some) of Our Afraffirmative™ Afrakan® / TaNubian™ matriarchal concepts, which I have coined and made publicly known since the early 70s, to help advance Our modern philasophy™ of Maatful™ Enlightenment; one which I have always known and have - through endless kultivation™ and "listening" to DivineShe™, been led to share with others. First through my visual ritual lexicon and symbolic artwork in the 70s; and later through clarifying the "Source" and ideological Principles in which my symbolic work is deeply rooted . . .

Use of trademarks has unfortunately become the only way to notify the unknowing that these particular concepts and words are NOT a part of some spontaneous social creation and that permission to use them needs to be obtained in writing -- and that their origin, lexicon, original meaning and intent must be retained and preserved, if and when use of these concepts is granted.

Over the last 3 decades, use of these terms have been intentionally misused / illegally used by some -- and others have simply attempted to change the content and meaning of Our words / language or worst, assert the origin of these words are their

own or belong to others, which has misled and confused the Truth of Our Good Intent . . .

So, while we earnestly understand that how inclusion of trademark notice throughout the body of this text can prove to be tedious (and may even seem unnecessary to some), we ask your kind indulgence and patience regarding this, until we find an alternative method of maintaining the origin, authenticity, tenure, SpiraKultural™ integrity, meaning of Our distinctive Afrakan® / AfraKamaatik® philosophy, lexicon and word-symbols . . .

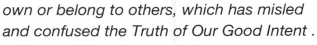 *Nehast Mas™ . . .*

2021 INTRODUCTION

About Our Approach: ReShaping™ WellBalanced™ Thoughts

"The first rule is to keep an untroubled spirit. The second is to look things in the face and know them for what they are . . ."
~ *AfraShe Asungi*

ike many other progressive practitioners, I affirm that therapy should offer something uniquely meaningful to each of our clients, if it's going to be effective in your lives.

As do most mindfulness practitioners, I too affirm that our clients will greatly benefit from successfully meeting two universal guidelines:

1) Face up to your own Inner-Most Truth (about whatever concern it is that has caused you to be where you are now).

2) Authentically make peace with (keeping an untroubled Spirit about) whatever it is that you're needing to face.

When we learn to tap into and ground in our unique Inner-Character Strengths to live in Authentic Truth with our Self and others; [which often means continually reassessing & challenging the disabling beliefs we hold, the peace-killing ideas we may have about our Selves and others] . . .

You will free your Self
when you learn to be neutral and
follow the instructions of your heart
without letting things perturb you . . .
. . .This is the Way of Maat . . .
~ Afrikan Spiritual Wisdom

When we're able to make peace with whatever we find there within us; then we will feel lighter, relieved, more contented and emotionally liberated . . . that plain and simply said, is . . . SistahPeace™ . . .

And here at SistahPeace™ ReShaping™ WellBalance™ Services, we're mindfully aware that we can accelerate any sort of desired SheChange™, growth and genuine sense of lasting wellbeing, by assisting you to ReShape™ and actively strive to meet these two basic goals:

Seeking Authentic Truth [Maat] about; facing and making Peace with those disturbing/ troubling/ stuck or derailed areas of our lives.

This applies, whether you're;

- •emotionally immobilized by a painful break-up,
- •depressed because you aren't able to find or maintain a healthy, loving relationship,
- •unable to admit or deal with your sexual orientation,
- •frustrated about your lack of much needed follow-through,
- •lacking direction in life,
- •can't stop unwanted or Self-sabotaging behaviors
- •unable to live your life like being happy is so much more rewarding than being perfect,
- •or just want to live a more authentic life, to be living your life "like it's golden".

During the course of our doing the reading and exercises in this Self-Workbook, you'll learn to develop and trust your intuitive insight and to affirmatively tap into your own uniquely SheInspired™ understanding and Inner Strengths, in order to become appreciative of the fact that you really can successfully bring an authentic sense of SistahPeaceful™ WellBalance™ and peace of mind back into your life . . .

. . . Fruitful Explorations™ . . . !

Always Remember . . .
And Strive to Actively Affirm . . .
That Living With Purpose
Always Includes Maatfully™ Loving Your Self . . .
~ AfraShe Asungi

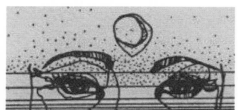

You'll have to make that decision for your Self. That being said . . . this Self-Workbook is intended for anyone who wishes to observe and participate in a modern and Womin-Affirmative™, Self-Transformation, Self-Awakening and Self-Affirmation Journey through Our 28 weeks of Self-Renewal, which is Rooted in ancient psycho-spiritual wisdoms.

More and more, people are becoming aware and are seeking to discover more about, and are actively practicing the increasing array of modern day Afrikan Psycho-Spiritual Sciences.

Many are seeking to do so as several of these modern Afrikan-Rooted Spiritual Traditions have become more and more socially mainstream and commonplace.

Particularly, those traditions, which are centered around the fact that the Ancient Mystical Teachings of Maat are the Original Source (Mamaroots®) for BOTH Western and Eastern Spiritual Philosophies and Religions.

> *"The Ethiopians say that the Egyptians are one of their colonies, which was led into Egypt by Osiris.*
>
> *They claim that at the beginning of the world Egypt was simply a sea but that the Nile, carrying down vast quantities of loam from Ethiopia in its flood waters, finally filled it in and made it part of the continent . . .*
>
> *They add that the Egyptians have received from them, as from authors and their ancestors, the greater part of their laws."*
>
> *~Diodorus, Book III*

It is promising that more and more of today's Seekers, from all corners of the globe are coming to be aware of, and are actively seeking to participate in the growing numbers of available modern Afrikan-Rooted Spiritual Traditions.

Unfortunately, only a diminutive group of today's Seekers have ALSO become aware that during pre-dynastik antiquity that the seat of the highest Levels of Enlightened Spiritual Advancement was rooted in the [now treated as if mythical] pre-dynastik Matriarchal TaNubian™ Mystery Schools, despite the publication and availability of my own work advancing that very Thought for more than four decades.

> *"AfraShe views Mamaroots® not so much as a pagan spiritual practice as a metaphysical philosophy. "The AfraKamaatik® Tradition is a pre-dynastic Nubian tradition, matriarchal and Goddess-centered." Of most importance is the code of standards that prescribes how members function with one another. This code is a modern translation of the ancient codes that were known as the 42 declarations to Maat, an ancient African Goddess of Just and Harmonious Truth.*

> *The philosophy underpinning Mamaroots® grew out of AfraShe Asungi's work as an artist. In the 1970s, she created a Goddess Series, "in which I created 10 African Goddesses, modern and traditional images, that started the discussion of, 'Is there an African Goddess?' and we evolved from there . . . I needed to see positive images of Black Wimmin™, and so I reached into the mythologies, the Herstories, and created the series in order to bring images to the present-day."*

> *Her African Goddess paintings provided the images that stimulated her developing philosophy, and her reinterpretations of ancient teachings. "My whole statement as an artist is that art makes change. Visuals are a way of changing and transforming the world. . ." "*

> *~ Home to MAMA™, The Company of a Priestess, by Lucy Jane Bledsoe, 1998.*

I have long affirmed [as far back as the early 70s] that I believe that the doors of Our last truly Matriarchal Mystery Schools of Ancient TaNubia™ were forced to close some 10,000 years ago, and that as the Priestess Order of these purely "sovereign" Matriarchal Temple Schools had either been co-opted, fled or went "underground", and that even those who spread throughout Afrika and the world, over time, found that their Sacred teachings were either eradicated, co-opted, disparaged or adapted by other competitive egalitarian, matrilineal or patriarchal traditions.

I have also [long] asserted that as late as 19th century, that the existence of these fragmented matrifocal™, egalitarian, and matrilineal traditions was rather easily found, not only throughout Afrika, but among other "earth-based" peoples, particularly in those very remote places around the globe [check out a few National Geographics from the 60s & 70s if you're interested].

In fact, a majority of those Afrikan people [who had been forcibly kidnapped and brought to the Americas as indentured servants and exploited slaves] survived the "American Holocaust" due to the fact that their belief in and practice of metempsychosis, "extended family" and matriarchal family patterns continued to remain intact [for the most part] until the 60s, when these "matriarchal" family structures [often headed by "Big Mama" or related female relatives] were systematically targeted and maligned as the reason for the "Negro problem" [meaning poverty and other systemic social inequities that have plagued the Afrikan American community since American "emancipation" in the 1860s].

Unfortunately, even in my own lifetime - I have witnessed the growing eradication of the [even back then] scantly remaining presence of any enduring matrifocal™ or

39

matrilineal traditions, which have been systematically annihilated, suppressed, or co-opted under global colonialism and other westernized patriarchal systems of suppression.

Systems which have methodically targeted most indigenous and earth-based, "non-westernized" people, so much that today, even the great-grand-kin of many of these "First People" have little knowledge that their Lineage Roots extend deep into these "lost" and seldom acknowledged [suppressed] Matriaffirmative™ "earth-based" traditions . . .

> *You are what you think,*
> *believe and Kultivate™ . . .*
> *And so it goes, that you BECOME what you dwell on . . .*
> *~ AfraShe Asungi, LCSW, ReShaper™*

Of course, Our own modern practice of metaphysically and Spiritually connecting to Our Ancient Mamaroots™ is deeply embedded in the original pre-dynastik™ Matriarchal TaNubian™ Mystery teachings. Meaning that the Sacred Texts of dynastik Kamaat™ [particularly Upper Kamaat™ -TaNubia™] left clear evidence and (symbolic) documentation that they [just like us] constantly re-rooted in, corrected, re-established, and reconstructed their own theurgy.

And they did so by referencing (even more) remote Matriarchal Theological Sources than their own, which they acknowledged as important Sources of Spiritual Wisdom Guidance.

And they [too] had to translate, reconstruct and adapt [usurp?] from these fragmented collections and "Secret" texts [which I affirm are from Our "lost" Matriarchal Antiquity] which they admitted were relics from very, very remote, and "Secret" [matriarchal] instructive theurgical texts; and which were often ethical and literary narratives, rituals and metaphysical prescriptions for maintaining personal, social and celestial Maatfulness™.

The Kamaatik™ temple theurgy [Enlightened practitioners, who summoned Divine Visions and Manifestations] were Guided to regularly "yoke" or ReRoot™ with these "Secret" instructive texts from their remote [pre-dynastik and Matriarchal] past, in order to maintain the Harmonious State of Maat.

40

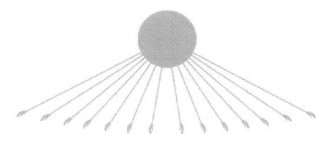

Even today, among one of the few remaining matrilineal people, the Asante [Akan] we can find this same Spiritual Precept of "yoking" / linking with the fundamental Wisdoms of the past to maintain celestial auspiciousness.

This precept is clearly reflected in the Adinkra Wisdom symbol of "Sankofa"; which while it has several meanings [as does most Afrikan lexicon] loosely means "it's not taboo to return and fetch it when you forget", and for purpose of this discussion, advises a "linking back" (Spiritual ReRooting™) in the Original Wisdom Teachings of the past.

Here again, we find this same Precept of materially and metaphysically yoking with/ linking back to (ReRooting™) in the original SheSource™, She Who transcends all material, physical, mental and intellectual comprehension, by Being (because She simply is) the Essential Source and energetic nature of everyone and everything (the Unlimited Oneness) in CREATION . . . which is center-most throughout the remote [matriarchal] texts of pre-dynastik™ Kamaat™.

Our Mama Maat, is yet another Ancient Fundamental Principle and Energetic Personification, Who was (is) center-most to the pre-dynastik™ TaNubian™ Matriarchal Mystery Tradition, as the Great NatraaMa™ (called Ntr by some) Who was the "One Eternal Kasmik™ Truth", Our Mama Maat is the "absolute measure" of Good Character, virtue and Harmonic Kasmik™ Order.

Therefore, Living by the Psycho-Spiritual principles of Good Character and Socio-spiritual Virtue was Thought to avert the weighted trappings of misery and emotional baggage (emotional pain and suffering) brought about by psycho-spiritual ignorance, selfishness and lack of Self-control (moderation) of temperament.

Our 28 week Self-Transformational process is soundly Rooted in these Ancient Matriarchal Dynamik™ Precepts of Being Metaphysically Rooted in and Justified in Timeless Maatful™ Awareness.

 *Nehast Mas™ . . .*

ReShape™: The Art Of SheAffirmatively™ Believing in Your Self:

A Womin-Affirmative™ SheChange™ Self-Workbook On ReShaping™ A SistahPeacefully™ WellBalanced™ Lifestyle

On ReShaping™ WellBalanced™ Thoughts

I Willingly ReShape™ My Thoughts
Knowing They become
My Feelings

I Willingly ReShape™ My Feelings
Knowing They become
My Words

I Willingly ReShape™ My Words
Knowing They become
My Actions

I Willingly ReShape™ My Actions
Knowing They become
My Habits

I Willingly ReShape™ My Habits
Knowing They become
My Patterns

I Willingly ReShape™ My Patterns
Knowing They become
My Beliefs

I Willingly ReShape™ My Beliefs
Knowing They become
My Character

I Willingly ReShape™ My Character
Knowing It becomes
My Destiny . . .

How To Get The Most Out Of
This ReShaping™ Self-Workbook

*"If there's a book that you want to read,
but it hasn't been written yet, then you must write it."*
~ Toni Morrison

*"Say to yourself over and over: "My peace of mind, my happiness, my health, and
perhaps even my income will, in the long run, depend largely on applying the old,
obvious, and eternal truths taught in this book." "*
~ D. Carnegie

ellcome™ to what will prove to be a life-changing excursion to
choosing to Kultivate™ you a healthier recovered, more grounded
you . . .

*After more than 15 years of working with Afrikan American Sistahs and other
Wimmin™ of Color™ (WOC) clients, I kept seeing a need for a workbook with
worksheets that were more aligned with the way I was working with them.*

*That deficiency has resulted in the creation of this workbook, which I trust will be a
helpful Self-help resource for others as well.*

*Many of my clients have reported, all too often, that they're habitually distracted by
other things. They seemed to be unable to regularly complete the readings necessary
to insure the positive outcomes they were sincerely seeking. They appeared to lack
the discipline to stay focused on regularly doing the more repetitive assignments
required in order to effectively SheChange™ the presenting problems into proactive
lifestyle solutions.*

47

As you will see in the following pages, I've selected to frame this Self-Workbook around our uniquely unequivocal Wimmin-Affirmative™ SpiraKultural™ Maat-Rooted™ approach, which I have dubbed "ReShaping™ WellBalance™"; combined with other post-modern psychology theories, such as Mindful Cognitive Behavioral Therapy (MCBT), Solution-Focused, Positive Psychology and other Afrikan-rooted, Asian and Wimmin-Affirmative™ methods.

Much like other 'Thought-centered' authors, 'who have come before me', I advise that, if you wish to get the most out of this Self-Workbook, there is only one essential mindset you'll want to make sure you bring to this process.

Simply speaking, it's a compelling desire to actually SheChange™ by regularly practicing, and an enthusiastic willingness to stop your current Self-Sabotaging Thoughts, Feelings, Habits and Patterns, in order to Kultivate™ and retain a proactive and fruitful lifestyle.

In the words of D. Carnegie, "Say to your Self over and over: "My peace of mind, my happiness, my health, and perhaps even my income will, in the long run, depend largely on applying the old, obvious, and eternal truths taught in this book." " 'Mirroring' Carnegie's proposals on how to get the most out a book, here's my own recommendations for how we can get the most out of this Self-Workbook:

> *1. Develop a deep, driving desire to 'Mistress' the principles of conquering your current psychological problems.*

> *2. **Read this Self-Workbook in its entirely at least once** before going on to select and complete the included Self-Worksheets.*

> *3. As you read through the material, stop from time to-time, to ask your Self how you can apply the recommendations.*

> *4. Underscore and write down any important ideas.*

> *5. Plan to review this Self-Workbook for solutions anytime you find any of the old Thoughts, Feelings, Habits and Patterns returning.*

> *6. Aim to apply any new insights at any opportunity which you can, plan to use any of the new perceptions in your day-to-day process, particularly as they apply to your identified problems.*

> *7. Be mindful on a daily basis, to assessing the progress you are making. Ask your Self what mistakes you have made, what improvements, what lessons you have learned for your future growth.*

8. Keep a "daily goals" journal as well as a ReShaping™ WellBalance™ journal, [use a 3-ring binder notebook to allow for flexibility to have both journals together] noting any insights, problems, Affirmations or positive outcomes which you wish to remember during these 28 weeks of actively learning and applying these SheChange™ approaches.

Proactive SheChange™ takes time and intentional effort; and so does SheChanging™ our Thoughts, Feelings and Actions. So, remember to be patient with your Self as you're learning to proactively ReShape™ your Self into the you that you Know and wish to be.

Dare to make a commitment to give your Self all the time and attention you need, without including the habitual negative Self-criticism. Strive to be kind and appreciative of your growing willingness "to make the effort" and put in the time to learn to increase your ability to gain and maintain a day-to-day Womin-Affirmative™ "peace of mind" mindset.

Our ReShaping™ Self-Workbook is Divided Into Three Parts:

In the first Part of this Self-Workbook, the focus is a brief explanation about the various psychological approaches, ranging from explaining the MCBT approach, through brief explanations regarding the included recommendations that you regularly practice mirror work, do the Self-regard exercises, Self-value assessments, gratitude, Loving-Kindness exercises, and several other "plans of action to improve my life" Self-Worksheets.

In Part Two of our Self-Workbook, our focus is to explain our ReShaping™ WellBalanced™ Thoughts approach. This approach is centered around our ReShaping™ WellBalanced™ Thoughts declaration, which typically is introduced outlined and reinforced via a framed poster as a means, to which I regularly referred.

And which is used as a way of assisting our clients to identify how, by learning that "Knowing that our Thoughts create our Destiny" thematic protocol will assist them in making day-to-day progress toward their ReShaping™ WellBalance™ lifestyle goals.

You may want to obtain and use an 8 ½" x 11" loose-leaf 3-ring binder to use as your journal, since it allows you to add, delete, arrange or rearrange sections as needed.

Please note that I've included in this Workbook a copy of our "On ReShaping™ WellBalanced™ Thoughts" methodology with a link to where you may get your own

11" x 17" color poster copy, since many of my face-to-face clients found it a very useful quick reference source as well as a visually pleasing decorative item. . .

Here's our Asungi Productions/ SheKultural™ Productions link: https://yhst-172736973-1.stores.yahoo.net/on-reshaping-wellbalanced-thoughts-poster.html

Part Three of our Self-Workbook is comprised of Twenty-eight Weeks of Proactive ReShaping™ recommendations and exercises, which are designed to foster a regular habit and weekly practice and repetitive use of a developing awareness of the various concepts which are introduced and explained in both Part One and Part Two of this Self-Workbook, as well as offering other recommended resources which you can use during and after completing this Self-Affirming journey.

Please initially begin by quickly reading through both Part One and Part Two of this Self-Workbook before you start to fill out or complete any of the Self-Worksheets.

Upon completion of your initial reading; which can be completed in as little as a week or as long as 5 weeks, depending on your reading pace; re-read both parts, this time completing the Self-Worksheets.

Along with your initial reading of the first Two Parts, please begin reading Part Three, starting with "ReShaping™ Week 1". It's recommended that you start on a Sunday morning and repeat re-reading the Weekly ReShaping™ and practicing the guidance for seven days.

And on the next Sunday morning, start reading and following the next Weekly ReShaping™ for the next seven days, until you've done so for all 28 Weeks. Remember to take notes as to any insights or Thoughts of any significance during this process.

Finally, it's also recommended that previous to beginning your second rereading of this Self-Workbook that you use the following exercise to reflect on exactly what are your intent and goals for this personal 28 Week ReShaping™ journey.

Honor the unique individuality of your needs and level of willingness to obtain them. Pause for a moment now to answer these three insightful questions:

1. What has brought you to our ReShaping™ Self-Workbook?

_____

_____

2. What are three SMART goals which you have for this process?
(for info, see page 249 - our Making SMART Goals Self-Worksheet)

    1._____

    2._____

    3._____

3. How will your life be better after learning to practice and using the Self-Affirming ReShaping™ approaches within this Self-Workbook?

_____

_____

_____

_____

May you be Blessed to live Maatfully™ every day . . .

PART 1

SistahPeaceful™ Thoughts Habits and Actions & ReShaping™ WellBalanced™ Self-Worksheets

"Women don't need to find a voice, they have a voice. They need to feel empowered to use it, and people need to be encouraged to listen!"
~ Meghan Markle

53

CHAPTER 1

On the Mindset of Learning To SheAffirmatively™ Believe in Your Self

"You have been criticizing yourself for years, and it hasn't worked. Try approving of yourself and see what happens."
~ Louise L. Hay

"ReShape™ your Thoughts into Maatfully™ ShePositive™ SheConsciousness™ and Actions . . ."
~ AfraShe Asungi

eveloping a Mindset of Learning How to SheAffirmatively™ Believe in Your Self

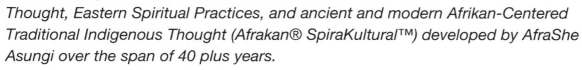

Our ReShaping™ WellBalance™ approach is an eclectic, Solution-Focused Womin-Affirmative™ blend of Afrakan™ SpiraKultural™, AfraUniThought™, Afrikan American New Thought, Eastern Spiritual Practices, and ancient and modern Afrikan-Centered Traditional Indigenous Thought (Afrakan® SpiraKultural™) developed by AfraShe Asungi over the span of 40 plus years.

While this ReShaping™ WellBalance™ as an approach is mainly designed to address Wimmin's™ Thought, Mood, and Behavioral disorders, it is also designed to address a particular deficiency in our ability to create and maintain a healthy mindset of SheAffirmatively™ believing in our Selves as Wimmin™. This Self-negating process and imbalance is more often seen in what we don't do than in what we actually do.

Stressful Emotional Mood Disorders of Which We Often Suffer:

Anxiety, depression, rumination, people pleaser perfectionism, Negative Self-Image, Disordered Thoughts. Some of the other psychological and emotional signs that we're "stressing out" include:

- *Depression or anxiety.*
- *Anger, irritability, or restlessness.*
- *Feeling overwhelmed, unmotivated, or unfocused.*
- *Trouble sleeping or sleeping too much.*
- *Racing thoughts or constant worry.*
- *Problems with your memory or concentration.*
- *Making bad decisions.*
- *Constant People Pleasing/ Being "nice".*

How We Proactively ReShape™ Our Thoughts, Feelings and Actions:

Putting this all into action. Did you know that recent studies show that 85% of what we worry about doesn't typically happen?

Most of my clients have already fallen into the mental trap of regularly experiencing negative thinking and spending time endlessly over-judging them Selves, dwelling on the past, or worrying about the future.

It's actually part of how we're wired, studies show that our brains react more intensely to negative events than to positive ones. That we are more likely to remember insults than praise.

Often, our Negative Thoughts spiral out of control. But CBT (Cognitive Behavior Therapy) and MCBT (Mindful Cognitive Behavior Therapy) informs us that these spiraling Negative Thoughts can be viewed as "cognitive distortions".

The CBT Approach

Cognitive Therapy (CT), or Cognitive Behavior Therapy (CBT), was pioneered by Dr. Aaron T. Beck in the 1960s. CBT is an umbrella term for a group of therapies and CT is a discrete form of therapy.

A number of treatments have developed that have been derived from CBT and are often labeled as the "third wave" of CBT by its advocates: MCBT, DBT, and EMDR are among them.

The CBT model is theoretically based on the idea that all external and internal stimuli are filtered through meaning-making, consciously accessible cognitive schemas.

The goal of CBT is to identify dysfunctional or maladaptive thoughts and beliefs [Cognitive Distortions], and replace them with more adaptive cognitive interpretations in order to have a more functional life.

CBT's Most Common Cognitive Distortions

Discounting the Positive: *Explaining all positives away as luck or coincidence.*

"Should" Statements: *Making ourselves feel guilty by pointing out what we should or shouldn't be doing, feeling, or thinking.*
"Ought to"
"Supposed to"
"Need to"

Perfection = imperfection
(Not being a mistake or failure, being worthy = being perfection)

All-or-Nothing Thinking: *Only seeing the extremes of a situation.*

Catastrophizing: *Blowing things out of proportion; dwelling on the worst possible outcomes.*

Jumping to Conclusions: *Judging or deciding something without all the facts.*

Overgeneralization: *Making a broad statement based on one situation or*

57

piece of evidence.

Personalization: *Blaming ourselves for events beyond our control; taking things personally when they aren't actually connected to us.*

Filtering: *Focusing on the negative details of a situation while ignoring the positive.*

Emotional Reasoning: *Thinking that however we feel is fully and unarguably true.*

"Awfulizing" and "Must-ing"
REBT includes "awfulizing", when a Womin™ causes her Self disturbance by labelling an upcoming situation as "awful" rather than envisaging how the situation may actually unfold; and "Must-ing"; when a person places a false demand on them Selves that something "must" happen (e.g., "I must get an A in this exam").

False assumptions
False assumptions are based on 'cognitive distortions', such as "Always Being Right", and "Heaven's Reward Fallacy":

Always Being Right:
"We are continually on trial to prove that our opinions and actions are correct. Being wrong is unthinkable and we will go to any length to demonstrate our rightness.

For example, "I don't care how badly arguing with me makes you feel, I'm going to win this argument no matter what because I'm right." Being right often is more important than the feelings of others around a person who engages in this cognitive distortion, even loved ones.

Heaven's Reward Fallacy:
"We expect our sacrifice and Self-denial to pay off, as if someone is keeping score. We feel bitter when the reward doesn't come."

Cognitive Therapy
CT is based on the cognitive model, stating that Thoughts, Feelings and Behaviors

(Actions) are mutually influenced by each other. Shifting cognition is seen as the main mechanism by which lasting Emotional and Behavioral changes take place. Treatment is very collaborative, tailored, skill-focused, and based on case conceptualization.

Rational Emotive Behavior Therapy (REBT)

REBT is based on the belief that most problems originate in erroneous or irrational Thought. For instance, perfectionists and pessimists usually suffer from issues related to irrational thinking; for example, if a perfectionist encounters a small failure, she might perceive it as a much bigger failure.

It is better to establish a reasonable standard emotionally, so the individual can live a WellBalanced™ life. This form of Cognitive Therapy is an opportunity for the participant to learn of her current distortions and successfully eliminate them.

In this ReShaping™ Self-Workbook, we'll be using ideas that are rooted in the ancient belief that Thoughts are the source of most folk's unhappiness and most mood disorders. That everything we are manifesting in our life started from a Thought in our own head.

This Self-Workbook was created mainly as a helping tool for our clients to continue learning how to regularly practice proactively "ReShaping™" their Negative Thoughts, which are at the Root of their current mental health problems.

It was also created to assist our clients develop and maintain ways of achieving a more stable sense of Womin-Affirmative™ mental Self-Satisfaction and Fruitful Self-Aboundance™. Given the focus of this Self-Workbook, it can also prove to be a useful Self-help tool for anyone seeking to enhance and stabilize her day-to-day Self-Affirmative thinking skills.

MCBT Simply Explained

*"We can all be Bodhisattvas by finding happiness
in the simple things, such as
mindfully peeling an orange or sipping tea . . ."
~ Thich Nhat Hanh*

The Mindfulness Approach

Mindfulness can be explained as the non-judgmental acceptance and investigation of our present experience, including body sensations, internal mental states, thoughts, emotions, impulses and memories, in order to reduce suffering or distress and to increase well-being.

Mindfulness meditation is a method by which attention skills are Kultivated™, emotional regulation is developed, and rumination and worry are significantly reduced.

During the past decades, mindfulness meditation has been the subject of many controlled clinical research, which suggests its potential beneficial effects for mental health.

Exactly What is MINDFULNESS ?

"Meditation is not evasion;
it is a serene encounter with reality."
~ Thich Nhat Hanh

The origins of the practice of Mindfulness in Buddhism

"Sati is a Pali" [Indian Sanskrit] word for "Mindfulness" or "Awareness". This Buddhist term which translates into English as "Mindfulness" originates in the Pali term "sati" and in its Sanskrit counterpart "Smṛti".

According to R. Sharf, the meaning of these terms has been the topic of extensive debate and discussion. "Smṛti" originally meant "to remember", "to recollect", "to bear in mind", as in the Vedic tradition of "Remembering sacred texts".

The term Sati also means "to remember" the teachings of scriptures. In the proper practice of right mindfulness, "sati" has to be integrated with "clear comprehension",

60

and it is only when these two work together that "right mindfulness" can fulfill its intended purpose.

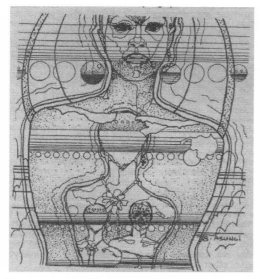

Traditionally, mindfulness is seen as an antidote to delusion, and is considered as such one of the "powers" that contribute to the "Attainment of Nirvana", particularly when it is coupled with clear comprehension of whatever is taking place.

And Nirvana is a state of being in which greed, hatred and delusion have been overcome and abandoned, and being so, are absent from the mind.

Mindfulness is essentially a State of Awareness which can be Kultivated™ within our Selves.

Today, mindfulness is a tool which is effectively used to help us master our Thoughts and feelings in order obtain more preferred outcomes.

Instead of (over)reacting to every passing Thought or feeling that we experience, mindfulness enables us to step back, and choose to non-judgmentally observe our Selves as we have that Thought or Emotion. When taking time to simply choose to be aware of our Thoughts and Feelings we gain the ability to decide whether we will or will not "believe them", and therefore decide just which actions or reactions are most appropriate.

We also learn to stop acting without making more Thoughtful choices. We also learn to be more accepting and compassionate in our reactions, as we separate our Thoughts, Feelings, and Actions from our own overcritical judgmentally.

In 2012, the American Psychology Association defined mindfulness as; "a moment-to-moment awareness of one's experience without judgment. In this sense, mindfulness is a state and not a trait. While it might be promoted by certain practices or activities, such as meditation, it is not equivalent to or synonymous with them."

Over the last 20 years, the term mindfulness has become a popular solution and tool in the psychotherapy field and has been noted in the research as being productive in the areas of resilience and well-being as well as in the CBT Approach to the degree that it has generated its own approach, which is aptly named MCBT.

The MCBT Approach

MCBT is taught within an overall cognitive understanding and framework. Research supports that MCBT results in increased Self-reported mindfulness, which suggests increased present-moment awareness, decentering, and acceptance, in addition to decreased maladaptive cognitive processes such as judgment, reactivity, rumination, and Thought suppression

MCBT approaches have been shown to increase Self-compassion; and higher levels of Self-compassion have been found to greatly reduce stress. The mindfulness approach is defined as a "moment-to-moment, Non-judgmental awareness". In addition, as Loving Kindness and Self-compassion increases it seems as though Non-judgmental Self-awareness increases as well.

The approach is very goal-oriented and is activated when the mind develops a discrepancy between how things are and how the mind wishes things to be.

The second main approach of mindfulness is the "being" mode. This method is not focused on achieving specific goals; instead the emphasis is on "accepting and allowing what is", without any immediate pressure to change it.

Most sources link J. Teasdale to the creation of MCBT, which promotes the "being" mode. This therapy approach was also co-created by Z. Segal and M. Williams and was partially based on the mindfulness-based stress reduction program, developed by J. Kabat-Zinn. Clinicians are also discovering ways to use MCBT to treat anxiety.

In becoming aware of our Thoughts, we gain some distance from them. And we give our Selves the opportunity to choose between being engaged with our Thoughts or not.

When we are not mindful, it's because we're basically not paying attention. It has been said that without mindfulness we go for and live on autopilot, depending mainly on our unconscious Thoughts, Feelings and Habits.

When we are not mindful we act without noticing what we're doing. Without mindfulness, we are often unable to focus or concentrate accordingly; and we get carried away by our Thoughts. We often act without thinking, and we are tossed all over the place by our Thoughts, Feelings and Actions as if we were humin™ puppets.

The Benefits of Mindful Practice

Mindfulness can help us become aware of our Thoughts and Feelings so that we can consciously ReShape™ our Thoughts, Feelings, Habits etc.

2006 research has shown that mindful practices such as tai chi, yoga, and meditation has shown that these techniques which train us to use our heightened awareness and better concentration and focus; often result in a greater ability to think about our own thinking, which is called metacognition. And with metacognition we come to realize the ability to detach from our thinking and then watch our Selves think about Thoughts that occur in our minds.

Mindfulness is not a fixed-trait, but an attitude which anyone can Kultivate™ mindfulness and meditation are related concepts but they are not the same. Mindfulness is a state of mind, while meditation is an activity. All the same, most researchers believe that mindfulness can be achieved through the practice of meditation.

As we learn to watch our own Thoughts, we also learn to avoid being consumed by our Negative Automatic Thoughts, we also learn to gain power over our thoughts, feelings and actions. We'll also come to recognize another unconscious pattern particularly for us Wimmin™, Thoughts of Rumination, and Habits of anxious over thinking.

When we become successful in mindful thinking we will also learn and use our power to choose how we'll respond in various situations. This of course will eventually lead to a greater sense of (mind-spirit-body) well-being.

In this context, well-being refers to a day-to-day sense of good mental health within a range of mental areas; such as greater cognition, lower stress and reactivity; mental flexibility and more satisfying relationships.

Where Self-awareness has been noted as disengaging that's from our Automatic Negative Thoughts. Mindfulness gives us a chance to learn to respond to emotional Thoughts and Feelings, and even choose to not respond at all sometimes. Because developing these abilities help reduce anxiety, depression and rumination.

Just to sum this all up, the research strongly suggests that there doesn't seemed to be an area of life in which adopting a more mindful approach doesn't improve our sense of life balance.

As far as psychology is concerned, the mindfulness approach is currently being used as an effective approach and so is CBT, along with positive psychology. Mainly because it is Thought that all of these approaches focus on improving mood, integrity, resilience compassion, joy and overall quality-of-life issues.

Self-awareness and mindfulness

Again, as was previously said, Self-awareness can be described as essentially mindfulness. An attitude of open, nonjudgmental awareness in the "here and now" is really one of the simplest mindsets for us to have, because it directly leads us to finding a more WellBalanced™ and Contented Sense of Self-Being.

J. Kabat-Zinn, suggest that there are seven basic pillars or humin™ attitudes which form the foundation principles of Mindful Living;

1. An attitude of non-judgment and non-attachment.

While there are a constant stream of Thoughts, we don't have to get caught up in them. Take a step back and withhold deciding on whether something is liked or disliked, good or bad etc. No need to analyze their value, just simply observe.

2. A beginner's mind

Be open-minded and receptive as if having a fresh new take on the things without being stuck into believing we have any expertise. Instead strive to see things anew in every moment.

3. Patience
Focus on the present moment letting things unfold at the pace in which they do.

4. Trust
Willingness to trust in our Selves and the great unfolding of which we are merely a small part.

5. Acceptance
While it is easier said than done, without any resistance, open to, and willingly stay detached from whatever emerges in this present moment.

6. Non-striving
Remember that there is no goal in meditation - we only have just Being. Remember to leave our egos at the door, while quietly observing the "Thought traffic".

7. Release into the Thought flow
Despite the never-ending flow of our Thoughts and Feelings, which watch over our awareness every second of every day; we can still get stuck on a nagging Thought and unhappy worry, or persistent fear. Choose to relax by neither choosing to, nor resisting the never-ending flow of our Thoughts and Feelings.

Tips for Challenging Our Negative Thoughts

Remember That Thoughts Aren't Really Facts.
Our Thoughts and Feelings are habitual, but they aren't always accurate. We might feel unacceptable, but that doesn't mean we are. Sometimes we can be our own worst enemies – other people may see us in a much more Self-Affirmative light than

how we see our Selves day-to-day.

Counter Negative Thoughts With Positive Ones.
When you catch your Self being mean to YOU, make your Self say something nice to balance it out. This may feel cheesy at first and Self-love can be difficult to make into your "norm"; so don't give up if / because it feels awkward to do in the beginning. Say and think things that you love, like, or even just don't hate about your Self – we all have to start somewhere!

Reframe your Self-Sabotaging Thoughts.
Think of a different way to view the situation. If your Negative Thought is "I can't do anything right," a kinder way to reframe it is, "I see that I messed up, but nobody's perfect," or a more constructive Thought is "I messed up, but now I know I can prepare more for this next time."

This can be hard to do this at a time when you're feeling down on your Self, so ask your Self what you'd tell your best friend if they were saying negative things about them Selves.

Prove your Self Wrong.
The things you think or do directly impact how you feel – what actions can you take to successfully combat your Negative Thoughts, to prove your Self wrong? For instance, if you're telling your Self you aren't smart because you don't understand how the stock market works, instead, learn more about a subject you understand and enjoy, like Art History.

When you feel like no one cares about you, call a friend. Give your Self direct evidence that these Thoughts aren't even true.

Acceptance of what actually proves to be true.
Acceptance in this discussion is the mindset that suffering comes not directly from pain, but from one's attachment to the pain. It has its roots in Buddhism and the psychological paradigm of Carl Rogers that acceptance is the first step towards change.

It's difficult to accept what we really don't want to be true. And it's even more difficult to not accept. Not accepting pain brings suffering. We often say, "I can't stand this," "This isn't fair," "This can't be true," and "It shouldn't be this way."

It's as if we think that refusing to accept the truth will keep something from being true, or that accepting the obvious means we are agreeing. Accepting does not mean agreeing, it means we accept a Thought, idea, reality, thing as being true, like it or not.

May you be Blessed to live Maatfully™ every day . . .

🪷 *Self-Worksheet 1:*
On Cognitive Restructuring
Our Distorted Thinking

About How Cognitive Restructuring Turns Negative Thinking into Positive Thinking . . .

CBT's cognitive restructuring technique is a good tool for anyone seeking to manage their unhappy feelings and moods. It's also a great technique to use when challenging your wrong-minded "Automatic Thoughts" that generate them.

Example: Tianna had just handed in a report to her boss. Lazoe read it and made a number of small criticisms about the results. Unfortunately, one of Lazoe's comments "touched a raw nerve" with Tianna, so she stormed to her cubicle, feeling exasperated and offended.

Tianna soon became aware that she needed to get over it, so that her negative mood didn't affect others. She eventually took a few deep breaths, and wrote down why she felt attacked by Lazoe. She then remembered that the overall quality of her work had actually impressed Lazoe, and that she had simply wanted her to improve a few items.

Tianna recalled how she'd also enjoyed working on the project, and, deep down, she'd felt she done a good job. After taking a few minutes to reframe the situation, she no longer felt upset. She called Lazoe to apologize for her over-reactive behavior, and then used her bosses' suggestions to improve her report.

Tianna has actually used cognitive restructuring here to overcome her negative, over-reactive thinking. We'll look at how you too can use cognitive restructuring.

Allowing merciless moods, as has been exampled above, are not only unpleasant, they can reduce the quality of your functioning, and they therefore undermine your relationships with others.

Cognitive restructuring helps you to change the negative or distorted thinking that

69

often lies behind these over-reactive, inappropriate moods. As such, it helps you learn to approach such situations in a more positive frame of mind.

Cognitive restructuring was actually developed by psychologist Albert Ellis in the mid-1950s, based on the earlier work of others, and it is noted as being a core component in Cognitive Behavioral Therapy (CBT).

Applications
According to the research, cognitive restructuring has been used successfully to treat a wide variety of conditions, including depression, Post-Traumatic Stress Disorder (PTSD), addictions, anxiety, social phobias, as well as relationship issues, and stress.

How to Use A Cognitive Restructuring Technique
It's ok for you to use the following suggestions on using the cognitive restructuring techniques below:

1: Calm Your Self Down
Use a deep breathing exercise or brief meditation to assist you in calming down if you're somehow feeling particularly stressed or upset.

2: Identify the Situation
Start by describing the nature of the event that caused your negative mindset.

3: Analyze Your Disposition
Next, write down the negative reaction, Thought or disposition, that you felt during the situation.

Here, our dispositions are the fundamental feelings that we have, but they are not our Thoughts about the situation. Research suggests an easy way to distinguish dispositions from Thoughts are that you can usually describe your dispositions in one word, while your Thoughts are generally more complex.

For example, "She trashed my project right in front of my co-workers" would be a Thought, while your associated dispositions might be feelings of shame, irritation, annoyance, or even Self-doubt.

4: Identify Automatic Negative Thoughts
Pause to write down your reactions, or the "Negative Automatic Thoughts," you experienced when you felt the disposition. In the example above, your

70

Thoughts might be:

- "She's so rude and Self-important!"
- "But my project is good."
- "No one here appreciates me."
- "Maybe my project skills aren't actually good enough."
- "She hasn't even liked me since . . ."
- "This really damages my future with this company."

5: Find Evidence of Objective Support
Identify some evidence that objectively supports your Negative Automatic Thoughts.

6: Find Objective Contradictory Evidence
Next, identify and write down evidence that contradicts the Negative Automatic Thought.

7: Identify Fair and Balanced Thoughts
By now, you've earnestly looked at both sides of the issue. You should now have the information you need to create a more reasonable and balanced view of what actually occurred.

When you finally come to a more balanced view, then jot your more proactive Thoughts down.

8: Monitor Your Current Disposition
You should now have a clearer point of view of the situation, and now that your disposition has improved. Write down how you feel now.

Next, pause to reflect on what you could do (if anything) about the situation. (By taking a balanced view, the situation may cease to be important, no longer need any further action.)

It's good practice to proactively use the CBT Restructuring Technique by going through the above process when you are experiencing a bout with your negative disposition, or when you feel fear, apprehension, or anxiety about a person or situation.

CHAPTER 2
How to Meditate

"The quieter we become, the more we can hear."
~Anonymous

*T*here are over nine popular types of meditation practices, and among them are:

❖ **Mindfulness Meditation.**

❖ **Spiritual Meditation.**

❖ **Visualization Meditation**

❖ **Focused Meditation.**

❖ **Movement Meditation.**

❖ **Mantra Meditation.**

❖ **Transcendental Meditation.**

❖ **Guided Meditation.**

❖ **Loving-Kindness Meditation.**

If you're puzzled about which of the above meditation practices might be best for you, here are four brief explanations for you, to help you begin to explore and consider which of the styles listed above may prove useful to you:

Guided Meditation
Basically, this form of meditation is one where there is someone leading you through a structured meditation session. Guided meditations usually come with music and with a theme, so they can be great for beginners and for folks who overthink too much.

Mindfulness Meditation

In this meditation form, one practices becoming aware of what is it now, without judgment or attachment. This approach to meditation is said to increase focus and decrease emotional reactivity helping the user gain a deeper sense of awareness and Self-regulation. It's best to set a firm time when using this approach.

Loving-Kindness Meditation

This meditation form is often used to generate feelings of compassion and loving-kindness towards your Self and others. This is also a good technique to use to help develop forgiveness towards specific people or the world.

Mantra Meditation

In this meditation, the user is given a special word to use for her mantra, which will be repeated to gently anchor her in the present moment. The word is gently used quietly or repeated out loud. We often see Wimmin™ using the word "om" as a term in mantra meditation.

If you have further questions about which type of meditation you might want to start with, further in this workbook will be a few links, so that you can try them out. If those links fail, just search on the Internet about how to practice the above meditation approaches listed here.

What is Meditation?

Often Westerners think that the purpose of meditation is to handle stress, to tune out, to get away from it all. While that's partially true, the real purpose of meditation is to tune in; not to get away from it all, but to get in touch with it all.

It's not to just de-stress, but to find that peace within, the peace that spiritual traditions talk about and which is noted as "actually passes all understanding". So, meditation is a way to "get in the space between your thoughts". According to ancient wisdom traditions, this space between the Thoughts, is the window, is the corridor, is the vortex to the "Infinite Mind", which is the Mystery which some Wimmin™ call "Spirit" or "Source".

D. Chopra suggests that we don't have to use those terms, but it's our Core Consciousness. And the more we learn about this space between Thoughts, the more we find certain things to be essentially true about it:

- *It's a space of infinite creativity, infinite imagination.*

- *It's a field of infinite possibilities – infinite possibilities, pure potentiality.*

- *Everything is connected to everything else.*

- *It is a place where something called "the observer effect", or "the power of intention", which means intention is very powerful when brought to this space, and it orchestrates its own fulfillment – what people call the law of attraction – so those are wonderful qualities of our own "spirit" or "source".*

According to Chopra, in meditation, the more we get into this space, the more we find infinite possibilities, infinite correlation, infinite creativity, infinite imagination, and infinite power of intention. And that's what meditation is really about.

Where to Meditate
When these are guided meditations, you can plug in, close your eyes, and go within in any safe place you choose, where you will not be disturbed. At other times, with other styles of meditation, it's best to find a safe, separate, quiet space, where you can sit comfortably alone.

When to Meditate
Morning and evening are said to coincide with our body's quieter rhythms. Our body knows how to be still; we just have to give it an opportunity. Studies show that routines begun in the morning last the longest, but any time you look forward to

meditating is the right time.

Body Position
Being comfortable is most important. It is preferable to sit up straight on the floor or on a chair to help kultivate™ alertness, but if you are ill or need to lie down, it's fine. The mind has been conditioned to sleep when the body is lying down, so you may feel a bit sleepier. Relax your hands on your lap, palms up or any way that you feel most open.

Thoughts
Thoughts will inevitably drift in and dance around our mind, but that's normal. Don't try to do anything with them, just let 'em be. If you find your Self thinking about what's passing through your mind, just return to focusing your awareness on the mantra or your breath; and you will soon slip into the space between thoughts.

Breath
When we pay attention to our breath, we are in the present moment. In an unforced, natural rhythm, simply allow your breath to flow in and out, easily and effortlessly.

Meditation Length
The effects of meditation are cumulative, and setting aside as little as 15 minutes a day to allow our Selves to go inside and renew is beneficial. Many schools of meditation prescribe 30 minutes of meditation twice a day, and as your meditation practice evolves, you can extend your time. It's better to spend just a few minutes meditating every day instead of meditating for an hour a week.

How Long and How Often Should You Meditate
If you have 10 minutes a day to devote to meditation, it's reasonable to expect it will be helpful.

Evidence suggests that 10 minutes seem to be a minimum amount of time for some of the benefits of meditation to occur. It also happens to be a very achievable length of time for many beginning Wimmin™ practitioners.

But remember if you decide to meditate for 10 minutes, on any given day once you hit 10 minutes, you can always continue to 20 if you're so inclined. The types of meditation which you can choose from is included a bit later in this chapter in our links suggestion.

For most of us, it's about how often we sit down to meditate, not how long. To help create a regular meditation habit, remember the following tips:

- *Start with a small "doable" plan like at "least 3 times a week". Keep track of how often you meditate. Mark calendar dates, or use a tracking app. This will help you hold your Self accountable without too much extra work.*

- *Remember, if you miss a day, it's fine! Part of becoming a meditator is having Self-compassion. Focus on how many times you're able to meditate in a week; or for the month, rather than on the one day when you did not do it.*

- *If you're falling short of your goals for consistency, reduce your daily target number of minutes of meditation. This will take off some of the pressure.*

Try these links to a few brief meditations focused on relieving anxiety and depression which you can start with:

> *1.Meditation for Anxiety - A Deepak Chopra Guided Meditation*
> *https://www.youtube.com/watch?v=hN-RsF17_Mk*
> *2.10 minute guided meditation for anxiety and depression*
> *https://www.youtube.com/watch?v=VDLfVwMSbJ8*
> *3.Guided Meditation for Anxiety & Stress*
> *https://www.youtube.com/watch?v=pxWOpGm4d7U*
> *4.10 Min Meditation - Positive Energy - Daily Guided Meditation by Deepak Chopra*
> *https://www.youtube.com/watch?v=5K5G7m112Vk*

Useful tips on incorporating meditation into your daily life regularly

1. *Learn to do quick 5 to 10 mins. meditations.*
2. *Practice right when you wake up or just before you go to sleep.*
3. *Practice short meditations during routine activities.*
4. *Let your mind wander without worry during your meditation sessions.*

May you be Blessed to live Maatfully™ every day . . .

CHAPTER 3

Mirror Work, Self-Worth Work & Loving Our Selves Even More

Let's affirm: Today I create a wonderful new day and a wonderful new future . . .
~ Louise L. Hay

lthough I was initially introduced to "mirror work" during the mid 1970s when participating in numerous Wimmin's™ Consciousness Raising Gatherings, I have selected to respectfully give homage to Louise L. Hay (who is most known for both her promotion of "mirror work" and actively loving your Self) by quoting her recommendations for doing Self-Loving Mirror Work here:

On Doing Morning Mirror Work
L. Hay suggests that we plan out just how we will begin our day with positive Thoughts and actions by following these writing prompts. Buy, and then take out that new ReShaping™ journal and pen and describe how your ideal morning ritual will look.

Creating A Positive Morning Ritual
Write down all the steps you will take in starting your morning routine in a positive, happy, and supportive way.

Say your "Good morning" affirmations. Then find and write down an affirmation that you can say for each of the steps in your morning ritual, review and consider your weekly ReShaping™ work next. Remember to meditate afterwards, and then do your

79

mirror work. Here's instructions on how you may do the following Mirror Work each morning.

Example of Morning Ritual Work

When you first wake up in the morning and open your eyes, say these affirmations out loud;

"Good morning, bed. Thank you for being so comfortable. This is a blessed day. All is well. I have time for everything I need to do today."

1. *Now take a few more minutes to relax and let these affirmations flow through your mind, then feel them in your heart and throughout the rest of your body.*

2. *Just before you're ready to get out of bed, take out your journal and review and write down any related Thoughts and Affirmation regarding your weekly ReShaping™ (see Part 3 in this Workbook) work.*

3. *Next, do a 10-15 minute meditation before you start your mirror work.*

4. *Then, go to your bathroom mirror. Look deeply into your eyes. Smile at this beautiful, happy, comfortable Womin™ looking back at you!*

5. *As you're looking in the mirror, say these Self affirmations: "Good morning, (your name). I love you. I really, really love you, exactly as you are. There are great experiences coming our way today.*

6. *Next, say something affirmative to your Self like: "Morning, (your name) you're looking good today. Your smile is fine . . . and you're gonna have an awesome day today"!*

When you initially start doing this mirror work, it may feel a bit awkward, even a bit silly, however over time it will come to feel as natural as breathing. Take your time and do this every day, even twice daily if you wish quicker results in naturally loving your Self.

Louise has been quoted as saying that in her opinion, "mirror work is the most effective method I've found for learning to love your Self and I have been teaching people how to do mirror work for as long as I have been teaching affirmations.".

And by now, you probably already know that another mental tool which is effective in enabling us in developing an authentic sense of Self-Love and appreciation is affirmations. Put simply, any positive Thought we say or think is an affirmation.

Any of our positive Self-talk; any optimistic dialogue in our head, are also streams of affirmations. Affirmations are active messages to our subconscious that establish habits and patterns of thinking, feeling and behaving.

Affirmations help us plant restorative Thoughts and ideas that support us in developing a positive sense of Self-confidence, Self-regard and in forming lasting peace of mind and inner joy.

The most powerful affirmations are those we say out loud when we are in front of our mirror. Why, you might be asking? Because the mirror reflects back to us, the (often obscured) feelings we actually have about our Selves. It makes us immediately aware of where we're resisting and where we're open and flowing. It clearly shows us what thoughts we'll need keep working on, in order to realize lasting SheChange™, if we truly want to accomplish an enduring mindset of a joyously fulfilling and SistahPeaceful™ life.

As we continue to do mirror work, we will become much more aware of the Thoughts we have, the Feelings we sense, the Words we say and the Things we do. We will learn to take care of our Selves on a deeper level than we've ever done before.

When something good happens in our lives, we can even go to the mirror and tell our Selves; "Thank yah, thank yah. That's awesome! Thank you for creating this." If something negative happens to us, we can go to a mirror and say, "It's okay, Sis . . . I love you. This thing that just happened will soon pass, it's a lesson learned, I love me, and that's forever."

Again, for most of us, being in front of a mirror and facing our Selves is challenging at first, however, as we faithfully continue, we become less and less Self-critical, and our mirror encounters turn into an emergence of "mirror play".

As we regularly continue to do our mirror work, they will like healthy seeds, fruitfully developing into new, healthy habits and peace of mind that also help open the door to a joyous and fulfilling life.

Again, it's so important to give our Selves, a whole bunch of never-ending, positive, Self-affirmative messages throughout the day.

The more we use mirrors for affirmatively complementing our Selves, positively approving of our Selves, and encouragingly supporting our Selves during those overtaxing times, the deeper, more gratifying and delightful our relationships with our Selves will become.

A Few Self-Love Habits Which Every Sistah Can Embrace

Here's a few recommendations that I found meaningfully written by A. R. Stewart, regarding our adopting a hands-on pattern of proactive Self-Love, which are advantageous:

She proposes that there's just no point in comparing your Self to anyone else on the planet, because there's only one you. Rather, focus on your Self and your journey. The shift of energy, alone, will help you feel uninhibited. So, ignore those voices in your head that say you need to be perfect. Make mistakes. . . . lots of them! This is fundamental!

She also suggests that (and of course, I concur) "Not everybody takes responsibility for the energy they put out into the world. If there's someone who is bringing toxicity into your life and they won't take responsibility for it, that might mean you need to step away from them. Don't be afraid to do this. It's liberating and important, even though it may be painful."

In truth, feeling afraid is actually natural and humin™. Don't ignore or reject your fears; instead, understand them. Striving to recognize your fears can help you in gaining clarity about the Thoughts that are actually causing you your anxiety. Learning more about your related fears will help you to reduce some part (if not all) of your anxiety.

Get into the habit of speaking your mind. Boldness is like our muscles, which grow as we exercise them more. Don't wait for permission to be heard, dare to join the discussion. Contribute your unique Thoughts, dare to take action, knowing that your voice is just as important as anyone else's. Practice proactively valuing and advocating on behalf of your own Self (Uhm-umn . . . meaning Self-Adoring Mirror Gazing, Dearest Sistahs™ . . .).

82

How to Proactively Love Your Self.

"It's a very simple premise—loving yourself. I've been criticized for being too simplistic, and I have found that the simple things are usually the most profound.," says New Thought practitioner, Louise L. Hay.

She also shared, "We don't know what we feel, we don't know what we want. Life is a voyage of self-discovery. To me, to be enlightened is to go within and to know who and what we really are, and to know that we have the ability to change for the better by loving and taking care of ourselves."

"It's not selfish to love ourselves. It clears us so that we can love ourselves enough to love other people. We can really help the planet when we come from a space of great love and joy on an individual basis."

"To me, love is a deep appreciation. When I talk about loving ourselves, I mean having a deep appreciation for who we are. We accept all the different parts of ourselves, our little peculiarities, the embarrassments, the things we may not do so well, and all the wonderful qualities, too."

"We are in the midst of enormous individual and global change. I believe that all of us who are living at this time chose to be here to be a part of these changes, to bring about change, and to transform the world from the old way of life to a more loving and peaceful existence."

Again, Sistahs, always remember that love is something we can choose, the same way we've chosen anger, fear, or hate, or sadness. We can choose to forgive someone who's hurt us, and then we can begin to finally reconcile. We can also choose to be grateful for what we have, no matter how little, or how much. We can choose love. Love is always a choice we have.

On Learning How To Love Our Selves Now

"The first rule is to keep an untroubled spirit.
The second is to look things in the face and know them for what they are . . ."
~Two Universal Guidelines

Sistahs, I have found . . .

. . . that there is only one thing that heals every problem, and that is: daring to love our Selves first. When Wimmin™ start loving our Selves more each day, it's amazing how our lives get better. We feel better. We get the jobs we want. We have the money we need. Our relationships either improve, or the negative ones' dissolve away, allowing room for the new ones to begin.

Loving your Self is a wonderful adventure; it's like learning to fly. Imagine if we all had the ability to fly at will? How exciting it would be! Let's begin to love our Selves now. . . and Dare to Fly . . .

Here are 12 simple but awesome strategies which I have adapted from the work of the Insightful "Thought Mistress", Louise L. Hay, which will help you learn and practice how to regularly love your Self first:

1. Stop All Negative Criticism.
Criticism never changes anything. Refuse to criticize your Self. Accept your Self exactly as you are. Everybody changes. When you criticize your Self, your SheChanges™ are Negative. When you approve of your Self, your SheChanges™ are positive.

2. Forgive your Self.
Let the past go. You did the best you could at the time with the understanding, awareness, abilities and knowledge that you had then. Now you are proactively growing and SheChanging™, and going forward you will live your life Womin-Affirmatively™.

84

3. Don't Scare your Self.

Stop terrorizing your Self with your Negative Thoughts. It's a dreadful way to live. Find a mental image that gives you pleasure, and immediately modify your scary Thoughts into pleasurable Thoughts.

4. Be Gentle and Kind and Patient.

Be proactively gentle with your Self. Be proactively kind to your Self. Be proactively patient with your Self as you learn these new ways of Thinking, Acting and Being. Treat your Self as you would someone you genuinely love.

5. Be Kind to Your Mind.

Self-hatred is only hating your own Thoughts and Feelings. Don't hate your Self for having these Thoughts and Feelings. Gently SheChange™ your non-productive, Negative Thoughts and Feelings.

6. Praise your Self.

Criticism breaks down the Inner Spirit. Praise builds it up. Praise your Self as much as you can. Positively Acknowledge your progress, no matter how little or how much.

7. Support your Self.

Find ways to support your Self. Reach out to your trusted friends and allow them to help you. It is being strong to be willing to ask for help when you need it

8. Be Loving to Your Negative Thoughts.

Acknowledge that you created them to fulfill a need. Now you are finding new, positive ways to fulfill those needs. So lovingly release those old remaining Negative Thoughts, Feelings, Habits and Patterns.

9. Take Care of Your Body.

Learn about nutrition. What kind of energetic fuel does your body need in order to have optimum energy and vitality? Learn to include exercise. What kind of exercise do you enjoy? Cherish and revere the miraculous temple in which you are blessed to live.

10. Do Mirror Work.

Look into your eyes often. Express this growing sense of love you are learning to have for your Self. Forgive your Self while looking into the mirror. Talk to your parents while looking into the mirror. Forgive them, while you're at it too. At least once a day, look into your eyes and say meaningfully, "I love you, [your name here], I really do love you!"

11. Love your Self. . . Do It Now.
Don't wait until you get well, or lose the weight, or get a new job, or find that new relationship you've been wanting. Begin now, and trust that you are doing the best you can.

12. Have Fun.
Remember the things that gave you joy as a child? Incorporate them into your life now. Find a way to have fun with everything you do. Let your Self express the joy of living. Be Grateful, Smile. Laugh. Rejoice, and the Universe rejoices with you!

During the course of your Self-Work, you'll learn how to develop and trust your intuitive insight and to affirmatively tap into your own uniquely SheInspired™ Inner Strengths, in order to successfully bring about an authentic sense of SistahPeaceful™ WellBalance™, a grounded sense of genuine Self-Worth, joy and peace of mind back into your life . . .

. . . Fruitful Explorations . . . !™

May you be Blessed to live Maatfully™ every day . . .

CHAPTER 4
Creating Healthier Boundaries

"In order to thrive and be successful,
you have to be able to set boundaries."
~ Oprah Winfrey

ays to Build and Preserve Better Boundaries
Understanding how to set personal limits is essential for building and maintaining healthy relationships. According to a Psych Central article, which stated that, "Many people know what the word "boundaries" means, but they have no idea what they are."

We might think of boundaries as something like a property line or a "brick wall" used to keep people out. But boundaries are not rigid lines drawn in the sand that are clear for all to see.

Boundaries are a way to take care of our Selves. When we understand how to set and maintain healthy boundaries, we can avoid the unhealthy feelings of resentment, disappointment, and anger that build up when we feel that our limits have been pushed.

Boundaries can take many forms. They can range from being rigid and strict to appearing almost nonexistent; which do you have?

If you have more rigid boundaries, you might:

- *keep others at a distance*
- *have few close relationships*
- *avoid close relationships*

If you have more loose or open boundaries, you might:

- *overshare personal information with others*
- *get too involved with other folk's problems*
- *find it difficult to say "no" to others' requests*
- *seek to please others for fear of rejection*

When we have healthy boundaries, we understand that making our expectations clear helps in two ways: we establish what behavior we will accept from other people, and we establish what behavior other people can expect from us. If we have healthy boundaries, we might:

- *share our personal information appropriately (not too much or not too little).*
- *understand our personal needs and wants and know how to communicate them.*
- *value our own opinions.*
- *accept when others tell us "no".".*

Many of us have a mix of boundaries, depending on the situation.

There might even be different boundaries based on a Womin's™ Kulture™. For example, some Kultures™ find that sharing personal information is not appropriate at any time, while in other Kultures™, sharing might be encouraged all the times.

Many agree that mental well-being is a key factor, as a lack of boundaries can "lead to emotional and physical fatigue," especially if you have to deal with the exhausting behaviors of others.

And it doesn't end there. Boundaries promote a sense of autonomy, that you are in control as far as possible, "in what you want and don't want." They can also "keep you safe in relationships at work, home, and with partners, and that's really important."

Start small and set them early

If we don't already have many boundaries in place already, the prospect of introducing more might seem overwhelming; so remember to build them up slowly. Doing so allows us to take things at a more comfortable pace, and it provides time to reflect on whether it's heading in the right direction or if you need to make some fine-tuning.

By setting boundaries and expectations from the very beginning, everyone knows where they stand, and feelings of hurt, confusion, and frustration can be lessened. Letting boundaries slide can lead to confusion and encourage new expectations and demands among those around you.

Try keeping things consistent and steady. This helps to reinforce your original limits and beliefs, and it ensures those lines remain clearly established.

In addition to setting our own boundaries, it's important to appreciate those of others, too, even if they're different from our own. So how can you determine what they are? It's also about using our common sense.

It might take us some time and consideration to translate the boundaries most important to us and the best ways to implement them, but our mental well-being will appreciate the effort in the long run.

May you be Blessed to live Maatfully™ every day . . .

CHAPTER 5
Expecting & Having Healthier Relationships

"If you continue to consider others responsible for all problems and difficulties, you cannot overcome your own problems and difficulties."
~ Hindi Proverb

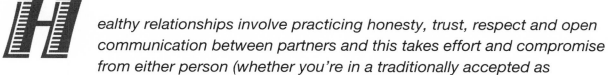

ealthy relationships involve practicing honesty, trust, respect and open communication between partners and this takes effort and compromise from either person (whether you're in a traditionally accepted as Western conventional, female with male tradition; or engaged in a more unconventional relationship, which falls within a LGBTQ+ community perspective, or within any other of the myriad "non-traditional" relationships, which Wimmin™ are boldly selecting as their ideal choices these days).

There is no imbalance of power. Partners respect each other's independence, can make their own decisions without fear of retribution or retaliation, and share important decisions.

Here are a few of those things that I've learned do seem to say something about "the strength of a union", and can be considered signs of a happy, healthy relationship.

1. You Speak Your Mind
Relationships thrive when couples can express them Selves freely and honestly. That means no topic is off-limits, and you both feel heard. Consistent

93

communication is vital to building a meaningful life together.

2. You Have Your Own Personal Space
Taking time to pursue your own interests and friendships keeps your relationship fresh and gives you both the opportunity to grow as individuals; even while you're growing as a couple. Just because you're in love doesn't mean you have to spend every moment together.

3. You Accept and Like Your Self and Partner as You Both Are Now
Healthy relationships should be based in reality. Chances are your relationship won't suddenly get better if you win the lottery, have a baby, or move into your dream house.

So, don't base your partnership on the hope that your partner will change. You recognize that neither of you is perfect, therefore, you both accept and value each other for who you are right now; not who you might one day become.

4. You Openly Disagree
Disagreements are normal between healthy adults, so if you aren't fighting, chances are you're holding back. But when people in healthy relationships fight, they fight productively and fairly.

It also means striving to understand your partner instead of trying to score points that means avoiding name-calling or put-downs. And when either or both of you are wrong, you kindly apologize.

5. You Make Important Decisions Jointly
Your partner doesn't call all the shots—neither do you. You're both willingly to make decisions together and listen to each other's concerns and desires, from what movie to see to how many children to have,

6. You Find Time for Laughter
Healthy loving relationships are filled with laughter and fun. This doesn't mean you're giddy every hour of the day; or that your partner doesn't drive you nuts sometimes; it does mean that your life together is mostly happy in sometimes very simple ways.

7. You Treat Each Other With Kindness
If you find your Self showing more appreciation and regard to other people than you show to your partner, take a step back and revisit your priorities.

Nothing is a stronger sign of a healthy relationship than treating the person you love with care, consideration, empathy, healthy boundaries and appreciation.

8. You Trust Each Other
Healthy relationships are built on trust and a commitment to communication without reservations or secrets.

9. Your Relationship Is Your Safe Place
Your relationship should be a safety net—a stable, supportive place where you both are pleased to come home to, at the end of the day.

10. You Say the Enchanting Words
You are happy to say, "I appreciate, love and value you." "thank you" and "I get it, and I'm sorry."

May you be Blessed to live Maatfully™ every day . . .

CHAPTER 6

Interdependency:
Not Doing Too Much Or Too Little

"Daily ReShape™ Thoughts & Feelings into Maatfully™ ShePositive™
SheConsciousness™ and Actions . . ."
~AfraShe Asungi

AInterdependency, *(also known as healthy dependency) involves a mutual give and take from both participants of a couple. Both folk willingly give and receive support, practical help, encouragement, and so on. But, in a codependent relationship only one person is doing most of the giving, but is not being given very much in return.*

It's critical to recognize the difference between codependency and healthy dependency. An interdependent relationship enables its participants to be their best Selves. Codependency happens when one participant is taking on most of the responsibility for the relationship, while losing her Self in the process by doing so.

When both folk in a relationship openly receive, and are given support, relational interdependency occurs. Each person can rely on each other to further their individual and mutual goals. In a codependent relationship, one person is doing most of the work and "rescuing" the other, to the point of neglecting and ignoring themselves.

Our present society is highly interdependent and specialized. We don't each understand how to build or fix a computer or a refrigerator, instead we rely on others to do this for us. There just isn't enough time in the day, to learn everything we would need to know, in order to do everything our Selves.

This reliance on others largely enhances our lives. Each person plays a role in enabling society in running well for everyone involved. Children depend on their parents for financial support, love, and guidance, which helps them grow into adults and claim their own special place in society. We are expected to interconnect and rely on each other for survival, friendship, learning, and to make our lives better.

In an interdependent relationship, there is mutual give and take. Both folk feel supported, respected and safe. Interdependency increases our Self-esteem and Self-confidence. It helps us feel like we can accomplish our goals more easily, and overcome our problems. Healthy dependency gives us the sense of support we'll need to go out into the world and mature into the person we seek to become.

In a healthy dependent relationship, we feel competent, yet still able to ask for assistance. We can develop a formidable sense of our Selves, respectfully expect and ask for our needs to be met; all while continuing to feel good about our Selves inwardly. We help each other in maintaining our own sense of individuality and in becoming and being the best person we can be.

Codependency

When we're codependent, our identity is wrapped up in our partner(s). We may not even know who we are or what we want without them. This kind of relationship is usually about power and control, resulting in a power imbalance. If we need to control someone else in order to feel ok, we're actively being codependent.

In a codependent relationship, we might be taking on too much responsibility for our partner's outcomes. The only way for us to feel okay is to control someone else. We don't have a solid sense of our Self as a separate person, so we look to our partner to satisfy our need to feel secure.

Codependent people often feel like we can't function without our partner. Blaming our partner for our own unhappiness, it's difficult to take responsibility for our Selves. We're just w-a-aay too focused on the other person attending to our own needs.

Instead of feeling happy and assured, we feel fragile and insecure. And too often, such relationships are controlling, abusive and unsupportive. We can become over-reliant on another person and lose our own identity. Instead of feeling that our wants, needs, goals and interests are being supported, we feel rejected, defective and undeserving.

The only way a codependent Womin™ feels worthwhile is when she's taking care of someone else. She spends all of her time fixing or rescuing them. One person in the couple is the "giver" and the other is the "taker". (Over)giving to her partner makes her feel needed and worthy of love.

When it comes to healthy dependency vs codependency, childhood neglect and suffering are often at the root of feeling fundamentally unworthy. If we have a healthy supportive childhood, we develop a feeling of Self-acceptance, feeling lovable at a deep level. Codependents, on the other hand, learn that the only way to feel loved is to figure out a way to earn it.

Early on in life, we learned that the only way to be valued was to give our parents what they needed. For example, if we made our parents breakfast, or prepared drinks for our parents. Or maybe we had to clean the house or dress a certain way to feel ok.

The point here is, that we had to work hard to be noticed by our "loved ones". We learned that the only way to feel any sense of worth was by getting others to validate us.

When we take our fundamental, deeply held (but irrational) core beliefs into our adulthood, they wreak havoc in our lives. Codependency becomes our habitual way of being in relationships because it feels "typical".

Our parents didn't know how to encourage us and nurture our strengths. For whatever reason, they didn't know how to help us feel accepted and loved for who we were, deep inside. We became too focused on them, instead of getting to know and "overstand" our Selves. This is how we lost our Selves and why we lack a healthy sense of Self-esteem

So now, we don't really know how to properly nurture and take care of our Selves. Instead, we find our Selves stuck in unhealthy abusive and unhappy relationships, and in a destructive pattern from which we just don't know how to break free. We just don't feel like we'll ever be loved if we aren't caregiving in some way, while blatantly neglecting our Selves.

We definitely aren't encouraging the other person to be an independent person because we are always "doing too much" for them. Instead of helping them do things for themselves, and empowering them to grow, we're stifling their development.

Proactively SheChanging™ such relationship patterns is very possible. With supportive, informative talk therapy, we can learn to identify patterns that don't serve us, and what to do instead. Learning how to set limits is key. Tools such as journaling, pursuing our own interests and, Self-affirmations are important, as well.

Understanding what healthy interdependency is vs unhealthy codependency in a relationship can be difficult. We have already taken the first steps toward doing so, by starting to educate our Selves and understanding just what healthy relationships actually look like; and then going out and proactively creating them.

May you be Blessed to live Maatfully™ every day . . .

🌼*Self-Worksheet 2:*
Commit to Proactive SheChange™

Wimmin™ are habitually known to naturally react to day-to-day unconventionalities with reactions of anxiety, distress, and even insecurity in the face of "unexpected" SheChange™. For example, imagine your Self regularly driving to work via the same streets at the same time every morning.

This is a set routine for you, and so you easily go through it, probably without very much Thought. Now imagine your Self when you are temporarily working at another worksite nearby, at a very different building, with a very different workstyle.

You probably feel a little anxiety as you struggle to quickly learn where things are and how they work, as well as searching among your things to locate the supplies you rely on and to prepare for your day. Whether it's positive or negative, dealing with sudden changes can absolutely be frightening and it demands a lot of you.

However, acknowledging your difficult feelings and working through them by committing to doing what it takes to accept pending options in your life can be intense and emboldening.

So, in this Worksheet, here's what you'll need to do. Write a Proactive Self-Commitment statement. Write your own unique statement, one which reflects your distinctive needs. Then, read, recite and review your statement as often as you need, in order to remember what you'll to gain from making daring Proactive SheChange™ now.

Here's a list of good examples of Self-Commitment statements:

• I commit to doing whatever it takes to make the Proactive SheChanges™ which I know I need and want to make in my life.
• I commit to focusing on what is good and positive about my Self and my life every day that I am taking on this difficult undertaking.
• I commit to embracing my fears instead of trying to avoid them.
• I commit to being patient with my Self as I try out new and unfamiliar strategies and interventions.

• *I commit to taking time for rest and relaxation, so that I have the energy necessary to complete the tasks I set for my Self.*
• *I commit to forgiving my Self for any setbacks or mistakes I may make on my journey.*
• *I commit to allowing my Self to receive the emotional support I need to help me throughout my journey.*
• *I commit to rewarding my Self every day for working to Proactively SheChange™ my life.*

Now write your own Self-Commit to Proactive SheChange™

I Self-Commit to Proactive SheChange™

_____
_____
_____

I Self-Commit to Proactive SheChange™

_____
_____
_____

I Self-Commit to Proactive SheChange™

_____
_____
_____

I Self-Commit to Proactive SheChange™

_____
_____
_____
_____

What do I stand to gain from committing to opening my Self up to a new way of thinking?

_____
_____
_____
_____

Think of a time when I Committed to make some positive SheChange™ in my life, no matter how small it was. What was it like? What would have made it better?

_____

_____

_____

What did saying my Self-Commitment mean to me? Did it in anyway impact my capacity to commit to my goal?

_____

_____

_____

_____

_____

_____

Is there anything in particular I've learned from doing this Self-Worksheet?

_____

_____

_____

_____

_____

CHAPTER 7

Regarding Self-Forgiveness

"Forgiveness is for yourself because it frees you.
It lets you out of that prison you put yourself in."
~Louise Hay

 elf-forgiveness is a form of Self-care because it releases us from the anger and resentment we often feel towards someone who we feel has wronged us.

Some Self-forgiveness suggestions are listed below, along with techniques, and activities that will help make it easier for us to forgive our Selves. We can be so hard on our Selves when we think we've "messed up". Far too often we harbor Self-reproach for our mistakes much longer than we need to.

We then start to project those Negative Thoughts onto others. Harboring such reproaching thoughts and feelings can also negatively affect our day-to-day productivity.

Our minds could quickly become consumed with our Negative Thoughts and feelings, to the extent that it becomes more difficult to focus on our daily tasks, and may even make us fearful of trying something we've "messed up on" before. Or even continue a relationship with a person who's previously hurt or deceived us.

Consider these Self-forgiveness tips to help us move on after we feel that we've "messed up". One Self-forgiveness definition is listed as, "showing ourselves grace and accepting that we've done something wrong". We can also say that it additionally means, "Self-forgiveness" is showing our Self compassion while separating our Selves from the past mistake(s) which we've made.

Why Self-Forgiveness Is Important

Some might wonder why Self-forgiveness is so important? Letting go of past mistakes is necessary, if we want to move forward in a healthy and productive way. Some folk may associate self-forgiveness with condoning the wrong action(s). But that just isn't true.

It's important to forgive our Selves, because proactively moving forward just can't happen until we've freed our Selves from the "stuckness" of our stubbornly holding on to the disappointment, anger, resentment, that comes with non-forgiveness.

We just can't be a "better us", until we forgive our Selves, taking note of the lessons we learned from our "mistakes", and proactively move on.

Identify your guilty Thoughts. Work to get down to the root cause of the problem. Apologize and then try your best to make amends. Release the shame associated with your mistake, reiterate proactive affirmations often, and let go of the mistakes that you've made.

Admit to these mistakes, learn from them, apologize to the appropriate folks and move on. If surrounded by folks who continue to throw your mistakes in your face, you'll need to be willing to distance your Self from them, until they are also willing to move past your mistakes. Remember, though, that you can't control other folks, you can only control your Self.

Consider what you would do differently if you were in the same situation again. Focus on your emotions. Identify your mistakes. Think about what you can learn from your mistakes. Understand that Self-forgiveness is a process. It's not going to be easy, and it's not going to happen instantly. Understand that you are not a bad person just because you made a mistake. Take the time you'll need to focus on your mistakes and proactively work through the Self-forgiveness process.

Here's some proactive actions that you can take to help make forgiving your Selves easier:

>*When you have those Self-Condemning Thoughts and Feelings; it's important for you to recognize when you condemn your Self over and over for that same mistake and replace them with positive Thoughts. Just as meditation is used as a form of Self-care, it can be used for Self-forgiveness.*

>*A Self-forgiveness meditation is effective because it allows you to positively*

106

(and verbally) recite and/or think through affirmations that can lead you to peace of mind. Here's a sample of a Self-forgiveness meditation that can be used:

"I recognize that I'm a Womin™ who, like others is an imperfect creature, and sometimes make mistakes. No matter how hard I strive, I am not and will never be perfect. My actions (or my intentions) have caused someone else to be hurt."

"I accept full responsibility for my actions and I will take the steps necessary to rectify my wrongdoings. Going forward, I will work hard to keep similar actions from happening again. I will not beat myself up repeatedly for this or any other mistake. However, I will make a conscious effort to not make this mistake in the future."

As you progress through the journey of Self-forgiveness, you may want to use others or even write your own affirmation that is more specific to your situation.

Journaling is a great way to start your Self-forgiveness journey. Getting your Thoughts on paper often brings clarity and you certainly need clarity as you work through forgiving your Self for a mistake.

When journaling, it's imperative that you fully express your Self. Don't hold back anything that you're feeling. Write freely in your journal, including as many details about the issue as you can. Writing in your journal helps you focus and can provide you with a better understanding of the mistake.

➢*The next time you make a mistake, and you're working through Self-forgiveness, try writing down the positive outcomes of your mistakes. You might be surprised to learn that your mistake wasn't nearly as bad as you Thought it would be.*

➢*When you are working on forgiving your Self for a mistake, you need to show your Self compassion. You also need to be compassionate towards others. It's pretty forthright to think of ways to show compassion to others.*

➢*Writing your Self a letter of forgiveness is a great way to fully express your thoughts concerning your mistake. Like journaling, writing your Self a letter allows you to get all of your negative emotions out and then move in the direction of amity. This letter could help you to better understand how you feel,*

107

putting you in a better position to move on, towards Self-forgiveness.

➢*Quoting Self-forgiveness affirmations can be very helpful on your journey to forgiving your Self. Here are some examples:*

- *I forgive my Self and am ready to proactively move on.*
- *I forgive my Self so that I can forgive others.*
- *I release my past so that I can step into my future.*
- *I accept that I did the best that I could at the time. Now that I know better, I will do better.*
- *I am loved and forgiven.*
- *Self-forgiveness is a choice. I choose to forgive my Self.*

Remember that Self-forgiveness is giving up the hope that the past could have been different. Give your Self a break. You don't need to be all things to all people or please everyone. Remind your Self when you're doing things well . . . don't wait to hear it from someone else.

Choose the brighter side of things. You can choose how to interpret comments and events, so try for the more positive interpretations. Accept compliments from others graciously. Look at temporary setbacks as opportunities for growth. Forgive and forget.

Try not to hang on to painful memories and bad feelings - this is a surefire way to encourage Negative Thoughts and bad moods. Your past can control you if you don't learn how to get past it. If you can, forgive past wrongs and move on.

If you have a hard time forgiving or forgetting, consider talking through your emotions with a good friend or a therapist. Don't dwell, it's important to work through things, but you can't let the past determine your future.

May you be Blessed to live Maatfully™ every day . . .

🌿*Self-Worksheet 3:*

Overstanding The Mindset of Forgiveness

Forgiveness is a conscious decision to let go of anger or resentment that we feel toward those who have hurt us. Forgiveness does not mean we've forgotten, minimized, or excused an offense.

Instead, it means recognizing it and making a conscious decision to let go of the pain. When forgiving another Womin™, it's not necessary to reconcile with her. We might believe reconciliation occurs along with forgiveness, but that's not always the case.

For example, we may be able to forgive a cousin who said hurtful things to us, but it might be too harmful (both mentally and physically) to continue to maintain a close relationship with her.

Forgiveness might take time, especially if the offense was a really serious one. When a Womin™ intentionally causes serious harm, true forgiveness can be pretty challenging.

Here's some suggestions to forgive anyone who has hurt us:

- Understand why the Womin™ hurt us by talking to someone we trust about the issue.
- Reflect on when we've hurt someone else, and treat forgiveness of another Womin™ as forgiveness of our Selves.
- Empathize with the other Womin's™ situation.
- Avoid focusing on the feelings directed toward the Womin™ who did wrong.
- Draw from one's own spiritual, Kultural™, and/ or religious teachings.
- Tell the other Womin™ directly that she's forgiven.

Forgiveness benefits us as well as the person we choose to forgive. Studies show an inability or unwillingness to forgive can have a negative impact on our mental health and well-being, contributing to depression and anxiety. If we forgive easily, we tend to experience increased happiness, better physical health, and stronger relationships.

109

In general, we are less likely to experience the negative effects of stress. We're able to resolve conflicts more easily, repair damaged relationships, and experience higher levels of empathy.

Forgiveness is viewed as an action, not a feeling. If we offer forgiveness, we'll likely feel a sense of relief, lightness, peace, and contentment.

However, these feelings will eventually come and go. In the past, we might have forgiven someone and felt good, only to realize later that our positive feelings have passed and that anger has replaced them.

What can we do? Feelings and emotions come and go, so that's why it's useful to view forgiveness as an action. You can choose to behave in a forgiving manner as our feelings come and go.

Do one action that is seen as creating a forgiveness ritual. We can use our creativity to adapt this exercise into something more relevant and personal. First, think of a time when someone hurt us.

Choose a situation that is still unresolved and where we've not yet forgiven the other person.
Describe._____
_____
_____
_____

Step 1. Complete the following statements: The Thoughts, Feelings, and Remembrances I have been holding on to:

_____
_____
_____
_____
_____

Holding on to these Feelings and Thoughts have hurt me in the following ways:

_____
_____
_____
_____

Step 2. In your own words, write a commitment statement that describes how you will let these painful Thoughts and Feelings come and go, no matter how many times they return—without holding on to them, getting caught up in them, or allowing them to cause additional hurt.

My commitment is to:

_____
_____
_____
_____
_____
_____

Step 3. Now, plan to read your answers from steps 1 and 2 aloud to a trusted family member or friend. Write down who you will read your statements to, when you will do it, and where you will do it.

_____
_____
_____
_____

Step 4. After you read your statements, do something that symbolizes starting over— for example, burn your statements and scatter the ashes. Write down what you will do.

_____
_____
_____
_____

Step 5. After completing the ritual, do something to nurture and care for your Self. Describe what you will do.

_____
_____
_____
_____

Reflections on this exercise:

After completing the forgiveness exercise, reflect on your values.
If you could respond mindfully when someone hurts you, acting on your deepest values, what would you say and do?
Are you willing to forgive, let go, and move on?
Are you willing to release your painful feelings and let go of unhelpful thoughts? Explain your answers.

_____
_____
_____
_____
_____

When someone you care about hurts you, how will you ideally respond?

_____
_____
_____

When you hurt someone, how will you ideally respond?

_____
_____
_____

What will you say or do to make amends?

_____
_____
_____
_____

What did you learn about your Self during this exercise?

_____
_____
_____

What else can you do to make and continue progress in this area?

_____
_____
_____
_____

CHAPTER 8
Self-Actualization

"Never make someone a priority when all you are to them is an option."
~ Maya Angelou

heoretically, well-being is defined as a maximum use of one's talents toward Self-actualization within one's potential. Psychologist, A. Maslow identified Self-actualization as the highest need in the hierarchy of humin™ needs.

Although Self-actualization is most often associated with Maslow, the term was first coined by K. Goldstein. Goldstein characterized Self-actualization as an individuation, or process of becoming a "Self," that is holistic (i.e., the individual realizes that one's Self and one's environment are two pieces of a greater whole) and acts as a primary driving force of behavior in humins™.

The work of another psychologist, A. Ellis, indicated that, "Self-actualization involves the pursuit of excellence and enjoyment; whichever people choose to desire and emphasize."

This focus on excellence and enjoyment as a symptom of the realization of potential explains the link between Self-actualization and well-being; if reaching your full potential is enjoyable and fulfilling, it logically follows that well-being will also be positively affected.

Multiple studies within the field of positive psychology have examined Self-actualization as a component of well-being, suggesting that it's a topic that is perfectly at home amongst the other popular positive topics.

Another more recent study by Maybury, examined the effects of a positive psychology course on well-being and found that college students who took a course on positive *psychology reported increased levels of happiness, hope, mindfulness, and Self-actualization, providing evidence of (at least) some sort of essential relationship between positive psychology and Self-actualization.*

It has also been said that, "Once we realize that Self-actualization is not about making the most money or achieving the highest status, that it is a desirable state, achieved through reaching one's full personal potential, we open the door of possibility in our own lives."

Self-actualization is about achieving our dreams, which means that it is within our grasp, whether that means becoming a painter, a politician, a philosopher, a teacher, or anything else that stirs our passion.

What Does Self-Actualized Mean?

Self-actualization can mean a lot of things, depending who's asked. One of the most broadly accepted definitions comes from Maslow, who described Self-actualization as the process of becoming, "everything you are capable of becoming." K. Egel, a San Diego therapist, simply explains it as being the "ability to become the best version of your Self."

You may be asking, "How do we actually become this best version of our Selves? And how'll we know when we've achieved it?" Egel says, "There's no script for that. Everyone has to find their own unique ways to hear the inner wisdom that can help them live a life of Truth."

In other words, only you can determine what Self-actualization means for you, but the following information may help to make this process of Self-scrutiny feel less formidable.

To cut through some of the uncertainty, it has been suggested that it might be more helpful to think about what Self-actualization isn't. Self-actualization doesn't involve perfection or things always going smoothly. We can become Self-actualized and still face difficulties.

In fact, a huge part of Self-actualization is recognizing our limits in addition to focusing on our "unique strengths"; whether they involve practical skills, artistic talents, parenting skills or even emotional insights.

Further, it would mean that you would live your life in a way that best utilized your unique strengths, while continuing to taking steps to successfully achieve your dreams, both large and small.

So, let's say a Womin™ dreams of becoming a famous pianist. She loves music, but can't really play a tune. Eventually, she finds that she's pretty good at playing the guitar and loves making music that way.

This Womin™ practices regularly, until successfully developing her guitar skills, and continues improving over time. Maybe she'll never become a famous pianist, but instead, she lives out her desire to successfully make music in a different way. This pretty much examples what it truly means to be "the best version of our Self".

There are a range of characteristics that tend to be associated with Self-actualization. Keep in mind that it's possible to have these traits (which follows) before ever reaching the point of Self-actualization.

Similarly, it's also possible to achieve Self-actualization without meeting every characteristic listed below. Generally speaking, a Self-Actualized Womin™:

- *Is comfortable with uncertainty. She doesn't mind not knowing what the future holds.*
- *Lives independently. She doesn't structure her life around the opinions of others. She may not seem swayed by social feedback. She'll also have an appreciation for solitude and won't always crave "the company of others".*
- *Has a fluid sense of reality and truth. She may seem more grounded and in touch with actual possibilities and have an easier time detecting falseness in others.*
- *Has compassion, kindness, and acceptance. This goes both for herself and for others she encounters.*

117

- *Has a good-natured sense of humor. She can laugh at her Self when she makes mistakes and helps others see humor in challenging situations.*
- *Has a sense of spontaneity. She lives more naturally, rather than in a rigid way, and isn't afraid to follow that which happens at the moment, instead of sticking to a routine.*
- *Is creative. Creativity doesn't just refer to artistic abilities. Some Self-actualized Wimmin™ might have a knack for looking at problems in new ways, or thinking along different lines than other Wimmin™ do. They may simply lack inhibition, another characteristic of a spontaneous nature.*
- *Enjoys meaningful friendships. She tends to build long-lasting relationships with a few folks instead of casual friendships with many folks.*
- *Focuses on things bigger than her Self. She tends to see the big picture instead of only considering her own life, and may dedicate her life to a mission, cause, or deeper sense of purpose.*
- *Has a compassionate sense of justice. She has compassion and care for all people, and works to prevent acts of injustice or unethical behavior.*

If this seems unachievable, remember that Self-actualization is a process, not an episode. There's no single point where we "should" end up on this journey. From a therapist's perspective, "Self-actualization is seen as a constant work in progress."

How to work toward Self-actualization

Self-actualization is an admirable goal to work toward. If we live our lives with meaningful purpose and authenticity and show concern for others, we're headed down the right path to be Self-actualized.

Self-actualization (much like Self-fulfillment) does not happen in one day, it takes time and conscious effort, and if we follow the appropriate steps and venture in continuing to, "Taken Action" to proactively SheChanging™ our daily practices, we can become more fulfilled with the simplicities of our life. Finding happiness within will positively reflect on everything we actually do; until we eventually learn to regularly "live our lives with meaningful purpose and authenticity and show concern for others".

May you be Blessed to live Maatfully™ every day . . .

 # Self-Worksheet 4:

SELF-ACTUALIZATION
(Overstanding The Mindset of SheAffirmatively™ Believing in Your Self)

Self-actualization is an approach that stems from an area of psychology, referred to as Humanistic Psychological theory.

Humanistic Psychology theory encourages us to look at the individual as a whole and places importance on concepts that support positive growth such as free will, Self-efficacy, and Self-actualization.

Self-actualization theory encompasses a core theme of humin™ existence: our search for emotional, physical, material, and spiritual fulfillment to achieve our full potential.

In Maslow's hierarchy of needs, it is the highest level of psychological development, where personal potential is fully realized after basic bodily and ego needs have been fulfilled.

The term, Self-actualization was coined by theorist K. Goldstein for the purpose of realizing one's full potential: "the tendency to actualize itself as fully as possible is the basic drive . . . the drive of Self-actualization."

C. Rogers similarly wrote about, "the curative force in psychotherapy, *(Womin's™) tendency to actualize (her) Self, to become her potentialities . . .*" to express and activate all the capacities of her Being."

And so, as humin™ beings, we have basic psychological needs for personal growth and development throughout our lives. By accomplishing self-actualization, we're able to find meaning and purpose in our lives, and we're able to say we truly "lived".

Self-actualized Wimmin™ are those who are fulfilled and doing all they are capable of. It refers to a Womin's™ desire for Self-fulfillment, namely to the tendency for her to become actualized in what she is, potentially.

Working towards Self-actualization is an ongoing process that will be heavily influenced by our changing life circumstances and developing experiences and needs. Self-reflection and Self-awareness is crucial to helping us work through this process.

There are many questions one could reflect on to encourage growth, development, and a better understanding of our Self-actualization journey. Here are a few just to help us test our own Self-actualization status:

1. In what ways are you open to new ideas and concepts?

    _____

    _____

2. How often do you take the time for Self-contemplation and Self-reflection? How could you improve this?

    _____

    _____

3. To what extent do you accept your Self and your life's circumstances?

    _____

    _____

4. What control do you think you have over what happens to you, and how you respond?

    _____

    _____

5. How do your current relationships help foster a sense of personal growth in your life?

    _____

    _____

6. Where do you see you could make improvements in your life to help foster a greater sense of fulfillment?

    _____

    _____

7. When was the last time you felt genuinely content? Where were you, and what were you doing?

   _____

   _____

8. How do you give back to others?

   _____

   _____

9. In what ways do you think you could make more time for the things that give you a strong sense of fulfillment in life?

   _____

   _____

10. How do you encourage and willingly bring new knowledge, thoughts, and ideas into your life?

   _____

   _____

CHAPTER 9

A Habit Of Gratitude:
Offering Deep Gratitude to Our Maatfully™ Guiding & Protective AnSistahs™

> *"I am an Afrikan, not because I was born in Afrika but because Afrika was born in me."*
> *~ Kwame Nkrumah*

Having a daily mindset of gratitude actually increases important neurochemicals. When our thinking shifts from negative to positive, there is a surging of, "feel-good" chemicals such as dopamine, serotonin and oxytocin. These have all been found to contribute to feelings of closeness, connection and happiness that come with having a consistent sense of gratitude.

In positive psychology research, gratitude is strongly and consistently associated with greater happiness. Gratitude helps us feel more positive emotions, relish good experiences, improve our health, deal with adversity, and build strong, healthy relationships.

It's true that Wimmin™ who regularly practice gratitude report having a better quality of life, and that they're also known to:

- Have less anxiety and depression.
- Be happier. Practicing gratitude increases feelings of optimism, joy, and satisfaction.
- Have better health. Studies have shown that the practice of gratitude strengthens the immune system, lowers blood pressure, and reduces symptoms of illness.
- Recover more quickly from challenges.

•*Have stronger relationships.*
•*Have stronger societal connections. Grateful Wimmin™ feel more connected to their community.*

How Keeping a Gratitude Journal Helps Create a Habit of Thankfulness . . .Maintaining a Gratitude Journal

1. *Plan to write in your gratitude journal every night for 5-15 minutes before bed. Set a reminder on your phone or schedule it in your calendar.*

2. *Keep your gratitude journal by your nightstand so you will see it before going to sleep and remember to jot down what you are thankful for.*

3. *Writing down 3-5 things that you're grateful for each day is a good number to aim for.*

4. *Your gratitude journal doesn't have to be deep. What you are thankful for can be as simple as "my family" or "a new novel or movie I recently enjoyed" or "Having great friends, who love me." or "What made me smile yesterday."*

5. *Learn to address your gratitude to your utmost ethical lineage and Herstorical AnSistahs™, "Those Who Open Doors for us", and proactively guide us to learn to make more Maatfully™ Rooted choices.*

6. *The timing of when you want to write is up to you. Journal when it feels right for you, the benefits really are worth it.*

7. *The longer you do this, the more it becomes ingrained in your subconscious as a new proactive habit.*

8. *Once gratitude becomes a part of your daily routine, your Thoughts will begin to shift. You'll become a happier Womin™ as you develop an "mindful attitude of gratitude."*

9. *Keep at it, continue journaling, and those new Proactive SheChanges™ become even more entrenched in gratitude.*

Habitually practice recalling, reflecting on, writing down and acknowledging at least 3-5 things you're grateful for every night, in order to simply make "being grateful" an innate, habitual part of your growing SheAffirmative™ Being.

May you be Blessed to live Maatfully™ every day . . .

CHAPTER 10

ReShaping™ Affirmations

"Change your thoughts, and in the twinkling of an eye, all your conditions change. Your world is a world of crystallized ideas, crystallized words. Sooner or later, you reap the fruits of your words and thoughts."
~ Florence Scovel Shinn

We really can learn to regularly ReShape™ our Negative Thoughts, Feelings and Actions into Self-affirming and proactive mental Thoughts and Habits that will enable us to remove those useless blocks of Self-resistant, resentfulness, fear-based Thoughts and Beliefs that are currently preventing us from having a daily joyously, Self-appreciative and Self-fulfilling lifestyle.

My own initial experience with written affirmations and a public articulation of the metaphysical viewpoint that "Thoughts govern our Destiny", was when I was introduced to the work of Florence Scovel Shinn. Shinn was one of the early known female artists and book illustrators, who'd become a noted, "New Thought" spiritual teacher and metaphysical writer (in some circles) who had, later become dubbed as, the "Mother of the New Age".

There appears to have been a revival of her works, as late as the 1990s and it's currently said that the work of this 19th century metaphysical teacher remains a formative influence on folk around the world, who are progressively being touched by her simple interpretation of this ancient Afrikan message, "that Thoughts are Destiny".

Around the years of 1962-64, as a young female artist, my Self, I discovered Scovel Shinn's book, "Your Word is Your Wand," (published in 1928). It became greatly regarded for its unbending "ancient Meta-Scientific leanings" and for reminding me to gain (and maintain) my own "Mistressry™" over my words.

At that time, I was also guided to study the all-too-few readily acknowledged Wimmin™ Artists, the Thoughts of Black Masonic teachings, and other female Afrikan-rooted Metaphysical Seekers, including those students of, diasporik™ and traditional incantations [spell-casting], in which practitioners turned "words into actions". In "The Game of Life", Scovel Shinn staunchly expressed her basic philosophy as knowing that:

> *"The Invisible Forces are ever working for (Womin™) who is always 'pulling the strings' (her)self, though she does not know it. Owing to the vibratory power of words, whatever (a Womin™) voices, she begins to attract".*

It goes without saying, that since that time I've come to recognize this ageless principle of "Thought Power" as a "Root Wisdom" in countless Ancient and modern "Schools of Thought" globally.

Ironically, it wasn't until I was working as a therapist in private practice in Long Beach Cali., in 2012, that I came across Louise L. Hay [who had also learned about affirmations from Scovel Shinn] and selected to use her more secular take on what had popularly come to be known as, "New Thought" principles (and writings) about the "Power of Thought", and the growing acknowledgement of her use of affirmations.

Louise Hay as a "New Thought" Practitioner

Louise Hay, as mentioned above, was an author, teacher, and lecturer who was well-known for her 1984 bestselling book, "You Can Heal Your Life". Hay survived many grim experiences, including sexual abuse and domestic violence, before she became a teacher of New Thought's, First Church of Religious Science.

By the 1970s, Hay had been diagnosed with what medical professionals called irreversible cervical cancer, and as a result, she began looking into non-medical healing alternatives for her as her option. In doing so, she advanced another lesser known approach in which she combined Self-Love, Thought Science, meditation, forgiveness, and dietary health.

What most appealed to me professionally, as a WOC therapist was her centering on the concept of Wimmin™ practicing Self-love as a

Way to restore the "imbalance" that caused the physical and mental disorders which we suffered. As an Afrakan® practitioner this was in keeping with foundational theoretical constructs and approaches, with which, I'd chosen to build my private practice.

In later interviews, Hay (who has same month and day of birth as I do), even shared how she believed that these approaches were what led to her being cured within six months of her diagnosis.

She astutely maintained that negative Self-perspectives and other negative beliefs are often the causes of our health problems.

Following her recently learned New Thought Path, she had reasoned that, through affirmations and other alternative approaches, like positive thinking, and healing Thoughts, that we have the power to transform our lives as well as our mental and physical health.

She has also been quoted as saying that in her opinion, "mirror work is the most effective method I've found for learning to love your Self and I have been teaching people how to do mirror work for as long as I have been teaching affirmations".

Another mental tool which is effective in developing an authentic sense of Self-Love and appreciation is (of course) affirmations. Put simply, any positive Thought we say or think is an affirmation. Any of our positive Self-talk; any optimistic dialogue in our head, is also streams of affirmations. Unlike Hay, I don't view Negative Thoughts and words as "affirmations", those I still view as Self "negations".

Affirmations are (positive) messages to our subconscious that establish our (positive) habits and patterns of thinking, feeling and behaving.

Affirmations help us plant healing thoughts and ideas that support us in developing a positive sense of Self-confidence, Self-regard and to create a lasting sense of Self-regard, peace of mind, and inner joy. The most powerful affirmations are those we can say are out loud when we are in front of our mirror.

Why, you might ask? Because our mirror reflects back to us the (often concealed) feelings we actually have about our Selves. It makes us immediately aware of where we are resisting and where we are open and flowing. It more clearly shows us which Thoughts we will need to SheChange™, if we want to have a joyously fulfilling and SistahPeaceful™ life.

As we continue to do mirror work, we will become much more aware of the words we say and the things we do. We also learn to naturally care for our Selves, and naturally take care of our Selves on a deeper, and a more meaningful level than we have ever done before.

What Is a Healing Affirmation?

This kind of affirmation is a positive statement about our physical well-being. Popularized by author and speaker Louise Hay, these affirmations are based on the idea that our Thoughts actually influence our health for the better.

We don't have to be sick to practice healing affirmations; this practice can be just as helpful for healing emotional suffering. Examples of healing affirmations include, "My happy Thoughts help create my healthy body," and "Wellness is the natural state of my body. I am in perfect health."

Typically, repeating such a Self-encouraging phrase allows these words of power to eradicate our worries and Self-defeating thoughts and instead, make space for Self-compassion and what I've coined as practicing "Maatful™ WellBalance™".

While they won't just magically erase anxiety and rumination, affirmations can counter our Negative Thoughts and Feelings of emotional distress and doubt, and bolster more positive Thoughts and Feelings of Self-Appreciation, Self-Love, enthusiasm and motivation.

On Listening to Affirmations While We Sleep

Typically, research has shown that affirmations really do "work better" while we sleep, because we attain a "delta brain state" and because our subconscious mind is activated and encouraged, making our affirmations more inherently effective.

To receive maximum benefits, it's suggested that we listen to our affirmations while sleeping for anywhere from 1 hour up to 7 hours.

Put simply, positive affirmations are statements used to challenge Negative, hurtful, or unhelpful Thoughts. That's how modern-day cultures are using them anyway. Affirmations help to reprogram the subconscious mind so we can believe the stated concept and make the SheChanges™ we need for the realizations we desire.

A useful affirmation could be a statement that hasn't happened yet, such as, "I am an accomplished writer", and by the time we've repeated it to our Selves often enough, we begin to think, feel, and act, as if it's fact. Over time, we become what we've been affirming and the power of Kasmik™ Thought naturally brings this scenario right into our experiences.

We can follow these suggested steps to create our own affirmations (only do so, after working with and using well-crafted affirmations, preferably some popular ones which were created by Hay or Schinn):

- *First take the time to identify the Self-limiting beliefs we want to overcome.*
- *Choose our affirmations using positive present tense. Begin with the words "I am" wherever possible. These are powerful words.*
- *Keep our affirmations brief and to the point.*
- *Always include an action word.*
- *Include a word that conveys emotion. This gets to the heart of our feelings about the outcome and makes it more true for us.*
- *Affirm what we want as though it's already true.*
- *Be grateful for it having occurred.*
- *Write our affirmations for at least 28 days, to allow us to focus on a single idea.*

133

Try Positive Morning Affirmations

According to Louise H., morning is a great opportunity to practice mirror work, in which we recite affirmations while non-judgmentally looking at our Selves in the mirror.

She also advises, that the morning is the best time to determine how we want the rest of our day to go. It's why positive morning affirmations can be very powerful, as well as a great opportunity to practice repeating them in the mirror. Here are some of her suggested affirmations:

1. I am beautiful and everybody loves me.

2. I feel glorious, dynamic energy. I am active and alive.

3. My Self-esteem is high because I honor who I am.

4. Life brings me only good experiences. I am open to new and wonderful SheChanges™.

5. Every experience I have is perfect for my growth.

6. Today I create a wonderful day and a wonderful new future.

7. Abundance flows freely through me.

8. Each day, I am growing stronger.

9. Today, I am tackling everything bravely and with confidence.

10. I am in charge of how I live each day.

SELF-AFFIRMATIONS, & WILLINGNESS RESHAPINGS™

DEEP GRATITUDE TO OUR MAATFULLY™ GUIDING & PROTECTING ANSISTAHS™

Daily acknowledge that life mirrors our mindset back to us; ReShaping™ our Negative Thoughts into Self-Affirmative Thoughts. SheChange™ your Thoughts, SheChange™ your Life.

Be open and receptive to creating a new attitude & then practice intentional kindness with Self & others.

Additionally, here are a number of our Willingness ReShapings™, that are from our own ReShaping™ resources, and are more specifically "aimed" at recognizing and helping to sever the too often denied, yet obstinate, internalized Negative beliefs by more effectively reaching into the unfathomable mindsets of we, WOC, where all too often, resides [secreted] persistently internalized Self-sabotaging Thoughts, Feelings and Beliefs.

The following Willingness ReShapings™ Identify a number of our idle Thoughts and fears and choose to question and proactively ReShape™ them into a new Self-accepting and more Self-loving, Compassionate, and Self-kindness mindset. Select those that apply to you and repeat them regularly to help you as you Proactively ReShape™ your resistant Negative Thoughts:

I am Blessed to be me, I love, like, approve of, and accept my Self exactly as I am.

I am choosing to proactively ReShape™ any Thoughts and Feelings of inadequacy and internalized Self-criticism into Self-worthiness and positive Self-regard.

I need not be perfect in order to affirmatively approve of, accept, be non-judgmental, and kind to my Self.

Stress is the result of fear-based Thoughts and Beliefs appearing to be real.

135

Gratitude triumphs over stressful fear-based Thoughts and Beliefs, I now release my pattern of habitual fear-based Thoughts and Beliefs.

I choose to ReShape™ my Negative mindset, which then SheChanges™ my Thoughts and Feelings, which then SheChanges™ my attitude about valuing my Self and what I believe I deserve.

I place my faith in prospering not in fear.

I replace any Self-limiting and Self-negating mental habits and beliefs with new Self-accepting and Self-affirming mental habits and beliefs.

I choose to attract solutions and release blame and Negative Self-judgmental patterns of thinking.

I focus on gratitude and know my SheChanging™ consciousness of growing loving kindness will prevail.

I am looking at the world and my Self with Loving Kindness.

I am kind to my Self today and will be aware of the Negative Thoughts that often scare me and misinform me that I don't deserve Loving Kindness.

I am releasing habitual Thoughts of Self-critical resentments and instead, am choosing to stop feeding any Negative patterns or Habitual patterns of Self-negation by simply choosing to replace them with growing positivity.

I willingly practice praise and support of WOC often, while developing the practice of kind and warm Self-regard by offering My Self Meaningful Good Heartedness as a growing habit.

I choose to gently ReShape™ old habits of Self-Negating Thoughts into loving Self-acceptance and prosperous Self-appreciation . . . only good lies before me.

I won't fear failure enough that it stops me from actually succeeding . . .

136

I am proactively finding and befriending other, like- minded folk.

I strive, kultivate™ and have the courage to dare to not be limited by the illusion of fear.

Repetition assists our mind in accepting newly forming habits. To the extent that we mindfully repeat new patterns we can successfully ReShape™ our lives.

Those age-old axioms are true, we are what we believe and do; where we focus our mindset, and beliefs is the reality we create.

The more we practice a new habit the quicker it becomes our "go-to" reaction.

We've gotten our current habits by thinking and doing them repeatedly. Repeated habits become patterns or even addictions, which over time create dis-ease and dis-order. Here are a few more Womin-affirmative™ assertions, which are Life-changing:

I can accept my Self and Be . . . Unconditionally me.

Yes, I Believe I can . . .

I dare to live my life Truthfully in Maatful™ Awareness. . .

My Life is exactly what I've made it . . .

I Like, Love and completely approve of my Self.

I always dare to take Womin-affirmative™ Action.

My energy always increases when I Say yes to my Self.

Divine Love now draws to me all that I need to make me happy and my life complete.

I have good health, strength, happiness, peace and prosperity.

Remember that 90 days of Proactively identifying and regularly ReShaping™ of our current Self-sabotaging mental habits, and persistently reoccurring, Self-critical mindsets (that have got us stuck in an endless pattern of habitual and Self-resentful negations) will result in real lasting and restorative SheChange™.

May you be Blessed to live Maatfully™ every day . . .

❧ *Self-Worksheet 5:*
MY PERSONAL VALUES
SheAffirmatively™ Believing in My Self

Personal values are "broad desirable goals that motivate our actions and serve as guiding principles in our lives". Everyone has values, but each Womin™ has a different value set. These differences are affected by an individual Womin's™ Kulture™, personal upbringing, life experiences, and a range of other influences.

List of Personal Core Values
- Adventurous.
- Authenticity.
- Commitment.
- Compassion.
- Concern for others.
- Consistency.
- Courage.
- Dependability.

What is a Belief?
Researchers state that, "A belief is an idea that a Womin™ holds as being true". She can base a belief upon certainties (e.g. mathematical principles), probabilities, or matters of faith.

A belief can come from different sources, including:
- A Womin's™ own experiences or experiments
- Acceptance of Kultural™ and societal norms (e.g. religion)
- What other Wimmin™ say (e.g. education or mentoring).
- A potential belief sits with the Womin™ until she accepts it as truth, and adopts it as part of her individual belief system.
- Each Womin™ evaluates and seeks sound reasons or evidence for these potential beliefs in her own way.
- Once a Womin™ accepts a belief as a Truth she is willing to defend it, then it can be said to form part of her personal belief system.

What is a personal value?

Values are stable long-lasting beliefs about what is important to a Womin™. They become standards by which a Womin™ orders her life and makes her choices.

A belief will develop into a value when the Womin's™ commitment to it grows and she sees it as being important. We can categorize beliefs into different types of values, examples include values that relate to her happiness, wealth, career success or family. A Womin™ should be able to articulate her values in order to make clear, rational, responsible and consistent decisions.

What is an Attitude?

Attitudes are the mental dispositions we often have towards others and the current circumstances before making decisions that result in actions of conduct. Wimmin™ primarily form their attitudes from their underlying values and beliefs.

However, factors which may not have been internalized as beliefs and values can still influence a Womin's™ attitudes when it comes to decision-making skills. Typical influences include her desire to please, sense of political correctness, convenience, peer pressure, and even her day-to-day psychological stressors.

The probability of such influences to sway her attitudes will be greater if the Womin™ has not clearly Thought through, and is not aware of her core beliefs and values.

A lack of Self-awareness or critical insight, or the presence of ambivalence or uncertainty about her values, can lead to a less rational attitude about her available choices, and could ultimately lead to undesirable behavior.

Examples of Core Values

1: Wellbeing

If you choose wellbeing as a core value, then you value the active pursuit of health as a priority, and the following day-to-day actions keep you on that value path:

- Pay attention to, and intentionally consume nutritious, healthy foods.
- Commit to doing enough regular exercise to stay healthy.
- Pay attention to your mental health by taking regular breaks, getting enough rest, and spending quality time doing things you love.
- Mindfully avoid Self-destructive habits.

2: Freedom

If we value freedom, then we value the ability to speak, think and act as a Womin™

140

without restraints. Some related actions that will prove affiliation with the core value of freedom are:

- Be open and free to express your Self.
- Be bold enough to create your own schedules and programs for activities.
- Foster relations with folk who support the path of freedom you're on and give you the necessary self-determination to authentically be your Self.
- Not being afraid of being your own boss.
- Have enough free time for your Self in your schedule.

3: Security

The core value of security depicts choosing a life path of safety, with little room for the unchartered waters and the unknown explorations. This core belief will restrict activities such as:

- Frequent traveling to new places for the spirit of adventure.
- Not seeking to set up a new business or join a new company.

Core values are designed to guide our decisions in our most difficult moments. Now you can intentionally explore them as you choose to proactively live the life that you actually want to live!

Self-Worksheet 6:
MY RESHAPING™WELLBALANCE™ PLAN
Creating Fulfillment in My Life

In our (ReShaping™) Lifestyle WellBalance™ practice together, our goal is to support and empower you to create a more fulfilling life and career. Please fill out the following scale to help assess your current situation and determine the most important areas to work on.

Rate each area from 1 – 10 using # 1 as the lowest level of satisfaction and # 10 as the highest level of satisfaction.

Career   _____

Significant Other   _____

Family   _____

Friends   _____

Physical Health and Wellbeing   _____

Emotional Health and Wellbeing_____

Physical Environment   _____

Finances   _____

Spirituality/Religion   _____

Education/Personal Growth   _____

Fun and Leisure   _____

Lifestyle   _____

Balance in Life   _____

Describe in more detail, the 1 to 5 areas in which I'd most like to focus on.

1._____

_____

2._____

_____

3._____

_____

4._____

_____

5._____

_____

If I could create the results I desired in these 1 to 5 areas, what specifically would I like to achieve in the next 90 days?

1._____

_____

2._____

_____

3._____

_____

4._____

_____

5._____

_____

What would I have to do or SheChange™ to make these things happen in the next 90 days.

1._____

_____

2._____

_____

3._____

_____

4._____

_____

5._____

_____

Self-Worksheet 7:
MY WELLBALANCED ™ LIFE PLAN

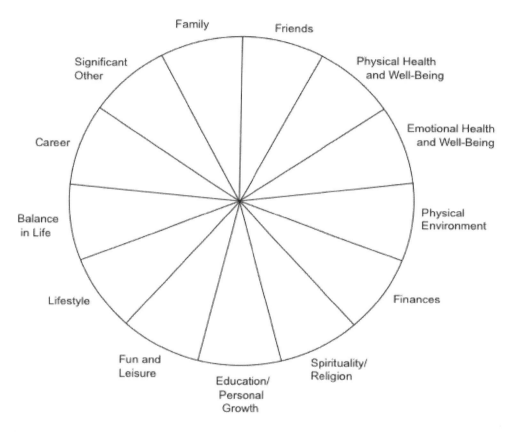

Question: Rate your level of satisfaction for each area on a scale from 1-10, where 10 is greatest satisfaction. Write the number in the "pie slice" for that area, or fill in the slice from the center outward, based on your rating, eg, for a rating of 5, fill the slice in from the center halfway to the outer edge.

CREATING FULFILLMENT IN MY LIFE

Please check those goals below that you would most like to focus on.

____*Clarify what I'd love to do*

____*Find a new job*

____*Start a new business*

____*Make a decision about which of the options I'm considering that I want to pursue*

____*Improve my present relationship, job*

____*Improve/ create more success with my goals*

____*Get a raise/ promotion or save more money*

____*Look at special life options that relate to a particular interest or talents, for example: All jobs that relate to writing, jobs where I can help children, work in the outdoors, work with my hands, etc.*

____*Focus on my life (SMART) goals and have a broader context for evaluating my life*

____*Other_____*

What is my timetable for making these SheChanges™?

_____

_____

What specifically would I like us to achieve in the next 90 days with my life?

_____

_____

What have been my last 3 successes and/ or life achievements?

1._____

_____

2._____

_____

3._____

_____

✤ *Self-Worksheet 8:*
WEEKLY SELF-RESHAPING™ FORM

1. What have I accomplished since our last Self-ReShaping™ session? (What are my wins?)

_____

_____

2. What I didn't get done, but intended to do?

_____

_____

3. What challenges and problems am I facing now?

_____

_____

4. What are the opportunities available to me right now?

_____

_____

5. I want to use this ReShaping™ Self-session to:

_____

_____

6. Insights and any new awareness which excites me.

_____

_____

7. Anything else?

_____

_____

Self-Worksheet 9:
LOVING-KINDNESS MEDITATION

Loving-Kindness Develops Over Time.

Loving Kindness (metta), is a traditional Buddhist concept, which implies acting with compassion toward all sentient beings, with an awareness and appreciation of the natural world.

"The giving of metta (an integral part of Buddhist medicine) has been shown as a way to enhance western mental health.", suggests one website. One way to enhance Loving-Kindness is to do a Loving-Kindness meditation like the following:

Your Position

Sit with your feet flat on the floor and keep your spine straight. Relax your entire body. Bring your awareness inward. Without straining or concentrating, just relax and gently follow the instructions. Breathe in. And breathe out.

Getting Loving-Kindness

Think of a person close to you who loves you very much. It could be someone from the past or the present; someone still in life or who has passed; it could be a spiritual teacher or guide. See that person standing on your right side, sending you their love. See that person sending you wishes for your safety, for your well-being and happiness.

Now bring to mind someone who values you deeply. Imagine that person standing to your left side, sending you energies for your health and happiness. Feel the kindness and warm-heartedness coming from that person.

Now imagine that you are surrounded on all sides by all the people who love you and have loved you. Picture all of your friends and loved ones surrounding you. They are standing sending you wishes for your happiness, well-being, and health. Savor the warm wishes and love coming from all sides. You are filled, and overflowing with warmth and love.

Sending Loving-Kindness

Now bring your awareness back to the person standing on your right side. Send the

151

love that you feel back to that person. You and this person are similar. Just like you, this person wishes to be happy. Send your love and warm wishes to that person.

Repeat the following phrases, silently:
  May you live with ease, may you be happy, may you be free from pain.
  May you live with ease, may you be happy, may you be free from pain.
  May you live with ease, may you be happy, may you be free from pain.
Now picture a relative or a friend that you love. This person, like you, wishes to have a happy life. Send warm wishes to that person.

Repeat the following phrases, silently:
  May your life be filled with happiness, health, and well-being.
  May your life be filled with happiness, health, and well-being.
  May your life be filled with happiness, health, and well-being.

Sending Loving-Kindness to Unfamiliar People
Now think of a casual friend, someone you don't know very well and with whom you do not have any particular feeling. You and this person are similar in your wish to have a good life.

Send all your wishes for well-being to that person, repeating the following phrases, silently:
  Just as I wish to, may you also live with ease and happiness.
  Just as I wish to, may you also live with ease and happiness.
  Just as I wish to, may you also live with ease and happiness.

Now bring to mind another female acquaintance, it could be a relative, neighbor, a colleague, or someone else that you see around, but do not know very well. Like you, this Womin™ wishes to experience authentic joy and well-being in her life.

Send all your good wishes to this Womin™, repeating the following phrases, silently:
  May she be happy, may she be healthy, may she love her Self authentically, may she be free from all pain.
  May she be happy, may she be healthy, may she love her Self authentically, may she be free from all pain.
  May she be happy, may she be healthy, may she love her Self authentically, may she be free from all pain.

Sending Loving-Kindness to All Living Beings

Now expand your awareness and picture the whole world in front of you as a little ball, which could be held in your hands.

Send warm wishes to all living beings on Mama Earth, who, like you, want to be free from all pain, contented:

Just as I wish to be, may we live with ease, happiness, and good health.
Just as I wish to be, may we live with ease, happiness, and good health.
Just as I wish to be, may we live with ease, happiness, and good health.

Take in a deep breath. Then breathe out. And take in another deep breath and let it go. Notice the state of your mind and how you feel after doing this simple Loving-Kindness meditation. When you're ready, mindfully go about the rest of your day.

Self-Worksheet 10:
MY PLAN OF ACTION FOR
Exploring My Personal Interests

What do I enjoy doing?

_____

_____

What were or are my favorite subjects in school?

_____

_____

What are my hobbies?

_____

_____

What kinds of books and magazines do I read?

_____

_____

What types of activities do I like to participate in?

_____

_____

Was there any activity I was involved in that I especially enjoyed? Example, volunteer work, community events, social functions?

_____

_____

What do I like to talk to my friends about?

_____

_____

 *Self-Worksheet 11:*
MY PLAN OF ACTION TO IMPROVE MY LIFE
Further Exploring My Interests

Exploring These Interests

THINGS I WANT TO RESEARCH, EXPLORE OR TEST OUT:

1. _____

2. _____

3. _____

4. _____

5. _____

6. _____

7. _____

OPTION TO EXPLORE: _____

3 - 5 STEPS I WANT TO TAKE TO INVESTIGATE OR TEST OUT THESE NEW CHOICES OR DIRECTIONS:

1. _____

2. _____

3. _____

4. _____

5. _____

OPTION TO EXPLORE: _____

3 - 5 STEPS I WANT TO TAKE TO INVESTIGATE OR TEST OUT THESE NEW CHOICES OR DIRECTIONS:

1. _____

2. _____

3. _____

4. _____

5. _____

OPTION TO EXPLORE: _____

3 - 5 STEPS I WANT TO TAKE TO INVESTIGATE OR TEST OUT THESE NEW CHOICES OR DIRECTIONS:

1. _____

2. _____

3. _____

4. _____

5. _____

OPTION TO EXPLORE: _____

3 - 5 STEPS I WANT TO TAKE TO INVESTIGATE OR TEST OUT THESE NEW CHOICES OR DIRECTIONS

1. _____

2. _____

3. _____

4. _____

5. _____

OPTION TO EXPLORE: _____

PART 2

SistahPeacefully™ WellBalanced™
Thought-Action-Destiny ReShapings™
& ReShaping™ WellBalance™
Self-Worksheets

"Women don't need to find a voice, they have a voice.
They need to feel empowered to use it,
and people need to be encouraged to listen!"
~ Meghan Markle

161

On ReShaping™ WellBalanced™ Thoughts

I Willingly **ReShape**™ *My Thoughts*
Knowing They become
My Feelings

I Willingly **ReShape**™ *My Feelings*
Knowing They become
My Words

I Willingly **ReShape**™ *My Words*
Knowing They become
My Actions

I Willingly **ReShape**™ *My Actions*
Knowing They become
My Habits

I Willingly **ReShape**™ *My Habits*
Knowing They become
My Patterns

I Willingly **ReShape**™ *My Patterns*
Knowing They become
My Beliefs

I Willingly **ReShape**™ *My Beliefs*
Knowing They become
My Character

I Willingly **ReShape**™ *My Character*
Knowing It becomes
My Destiny *. . .*

CHAPTER 11

About Our ReShaping™ WellBalanced™ Thoughts Pledge

Many folks globally, are coming to recognize, that our Thoughts are nothing more than an endless stream of ideas running through our minds. Our Thoughts are mostly powerless until we (consciously or unconsciously) decide to attach to and obsess over one of them. Whichever Thought you choose to focus on and plant, it will then grow and multiply.

We are the Kultivators™ of these Thought seeds which mature into realization and actions that determine our life's destiny. We create our Thought patterns, which become what psychologists call "metacognition", the idea of our thinking about our thinking.

1. We can choose to increase our awareness by observing our emotions and body reactions.
2. Be more conscious of what Thoughts we give our attention to.

Once we agree to give our attention to a Thought, it becomes more and more real to us over time and gains more and more power over our lives. It elicits an emotion, which activates a body reaction and drives us to act in a certain way.

This Thought pattern creates a mental circuit in our brain, and as we repeat it, it becomes a subconscious pattern that runs instinctively.

This is how our Thoughts actually structure our reality. This is why we are what we think. And this is why the great thinkers agree that: "We live in a world of (our own and other's) Thoughts."

Simply said, our Thoughts create our experiences, and thus, we experience what we think. The quality of our Thoughts then creates the quality of our life.

Repeating this awareness helps us "think about what we choose to think about", change and direct it and eventually gain control over what we repetitively chose to think, do, act on, believe and become.

Of course, you may use this reproduction or a poster of it, so that you can hang it, in order to habitually read it and review these ideas often.

Use it to consistently remind your Self to mindfully be aware of which Thoughts you choose to focus your attention on. They become your beliefs and they go on to define your life and how you experience it.

. . . Our Thoughts Determine Our Destiny . . .

An 11" x 17" sized color poster of this Life-Affirming Declaration can be purchased.

Please see our "Thanks page" for more info on how to do so.

May you be Blessed to live Maatfully™ every day . . .

CHAPTER 12

About Our Willingly ReShaping™ WellBalanced™ Thoughts

hat Exactly is a Thought?

Generally speaking, a' Thought[1] is an, "idea, notion, opinion, view, impression, feeling, theory; it's also a judgment, assessment, conclusion." It is also defined as being, "the action or process of thinking"; as in, "Sophie sat deep in Thought."

Thought is also defined as, encompassing an "aim-free flow of ideas and associations that can lead to a reality-oriented conclusion." Wikipedia says, "Although thinking is an activity of an existential value for humans, there is no consensus as to how it is defined or understood."

Thoughts and Feelings.

The first distinction we need to make is that feelings, as the word is used here, means emotions. Secondly, feelings are not the same as Thoughts, even though we commonly hear them spoken of that way. Actually, Thoughts and Feelings are experienced in very different areas of the brain. In short, it's easy to look at Feelings as emotional Thoughts, which often cause emotional over-reactions.

Whether learned while in therapy, or on your own, cognitive restructuring is a MCBT technique that involves a step-by-step process in which our Negative Thoughts are identified, assessed for their accuracy, and Thoughtfully replaced.

While it is often initially challenging to learn this new technique at first, with regular practice, reasonable and positive Thoughts will come to us more naturally.

167

"Acceptance is a big issue in another CBT approach, REBT. The three cornerstones of REBT are:

> *1.) "unconditional Self-acceptance,"*
> *2.) "unconditional other acceptance,"*
> *3.) "unconditional life acceptance."*

As REBT founder, Ellis would say, "Your mother never told you she loved you? That's her right as a "fallible f-cked-up human,", and often does. There are worse things in life than not being told you're loved by your mother, he argues."

He also taught, "Don't "awfulize" such neglect; use rational thinking to understand that another person's poor behavior has nothing to do with your sense of identity or potential for happiness."

Ellis, who was noted as an avid reader of philosophy in his teens, credits Epictetus with steering him toward the guiding principle that our emotional responses to upsetting actions; not the actions them Selves; are what create anxiety and depression. And if we construct our unhappiness, then, REBT's reasoning goes, we can also break it apart."

REBT research about shows us that, with very invasive Thoughts we may have to do the above steps several times in a row each time the intrusive Thoughts grab a hold of us.

Once we remove our emotional response to invasive Thoughts, we tend to "normalize them" and they no longer have an emotional pull on us. When they no longer have a pull, they fall away by themselves naturally because they no longer have anything to cling onto.

We Are Not Our Thoughts

These invasive Thoughts don't represent the real us. They're just the result of our creative imaginations jumbled up with anxiety and fatigue. In fact, rather than beating our Selves up over them, we can use our Thoughts as guide-posts, as popular visual cues similar to how they're used in Mindful Cognitive Behavioral Therapy.

As we work through the following "ReShaping™ WellBalanced™ Thoughts" chapters within Part 2 of this Self-Workbook, (which are designed to follow and ReShape™ this notion that shows us just how it is that our Thoughts determine our Destiny), we will effectively learn to better manage our Thoughts, Feelings and Actions, we will naturally gain the ability to sensibly direct and govern our Destiny.

May you be Blessed to live Maatfully™ every day . . .

Self-Worksheet 12:
Identifying, Challenging,
and SheChanging™ Negative Self-Talk

How is Negative Self-Talk Related To Negative Automatic Thoughts?

Your Self-talk, whether you are aware of it or not, either sabotages (negative) or supports (positive) you. Negative Self-talk can result in unnecessary stress, anxiety, panic, depression, Self-doubt, etc.

Positive Self-talk encourages Self-confidence, effective coping, achievement, and a general feeling of well-being. So, ask your Self, "Are my Thoughts reasonable or irrational?" "Is my Self-talk building me up or tearing me down?" "Is my way of thinking helping me or is it hindering me?".

Instructions

1. Think of a recent time when you were experiencing negative or unhelpful Thoughts.
   - What was the situation?
   - How did you feel?
   - What did you do?

2. Now, use this step-by-step guide and see if changing the way you think could possibly bring a better result.

3. Given what you have reviewed here, what is one thing you are willing to start doing that can help you better manage your negative thinking?

Changing Your Self-Talk
- Catch it. Recognize when you are having negative or unhelpful Thoughts.
- Control it. Stop! When you find your Self thinking negatively, just gently say STOP to your Self (silently) to stop the downward spiral of Thoughts leading to sadness, guilt, anxiety, self-doubt, hurt, resentment, etc.

171

- *Self-Challenge it. Challenge what you are saying to your Self using the various questions below.*
- *Change it. Change the negative messages you are saying to your Self to more realistic/ positive ones in order to bring about more pleasant and helpful emotions.*
- *Cherish it. Enjoy the moment and the feeling you have just created!*

Challenging Your Thoughts

- *Is this Thought helpful? What is a healthier Thought?*
- *What would I tell a friend in this situation? (should I now follow this advice?)*
- *What evidence do I have that what I'm thinking is really true? What is the evidence against it?*
- *Is there any other reason this situation could have occurred?*
- *Is there another way of looking at this situation? What are some other points-of-view?*
- *What is the worst/ best/ most likely outcome? If the worst did happen, how could I cope? Would I live through it?*
- *Is there anything I can do about this right now? If yes, take appropriate action. If no, accept it and move on.*

When faced with a problem we can choose to respond carefully by thinking of possible solutions and then examining the advantages and disadvantages of each, or we might just have a quick and automatic hunch about how to solve it. It turns out that our brains are surprisingly lazy and bias often creeps into our thinking.

Key Things That You Need To Know Are:

- *We all have quick and automatic Thoughts that just 'pop' into our minds*
- *These automatic Thoughts are often based on assumptions.*
- *Automatic Thoughts are often very believable, but they can be inaccurate.*
- *In summary, Thoughts are not facts.*

Event: Thought: Emotion:

_____   _____   _____

_____   _____   _____

_____   _____   _____

_____   _____   _____

172

Evidence for my Thought   Evidence against my Thought

_____   _____

_____   _____

_____   _____

_____   _____

Remember to consider the following points in your examination of the evidence:

1. Am I ignoring any evidence that would contradict my Thoughts?

2. How likely is it that I'm seeing it as worse than it really is?

3. What would I say to someone I care about if they had this Thought?

Based on my examination of the evidence, would I revise my Thought in any way to better fit the evidence I came up with?
If so, write it below.

A more reality-based Thought is: _____

_____

_____

_____

Based on the evidence that I've reviewed, how accurate is my Thought ?

_____

_____

_____

_____

How would I modify my Thought to make it fit better with reality?

_____

_____

_____

🌾 *Self-Worksheet 13:*
MCBT Thought Log
ReShaping™ My Negative Thoughts 1

A "Thought" log is a fundamental tool in Mindful Cognitive Behavioral Therapy (MCBT). The underlying principle can be summarized as "what do you believe, and why do you believe it?".

> This Thought log can be used to:
> Identify Negative Automatic Thoughts (NATs) and.
> Help understand the links between Thoughts and Emotions.
> Examine the evidence for and against a selected NAT.
> Challenge and generate more realistic alternatives to a NAT.

The cue for completing a Thought log is usually a sudden change in emotion. In the question below write the emotion felt and its' subjective intensity.

1. Start with a situation / event. What happened? Where? When? Who with? How?

_____

_____

_____

Emotion _____

2. What were the Automatic Thoughts

_____

_____

_____

Emotion _____

3. Which distressing Thoughts did you automatically have after the event?

_____

_____

_____

Emotion _____

4. Rate feelings and emotions (Rate 0-100%)

What emotion did I feel at that time? What else? How intense was it? What did I notice in my body? Where did I feel it?

_____

_____

_____

_____

_____

_____

Emotion _____

5. Identify what destructive thinking pattern you had for each Automatic Thought. Enter destructive thinking patterns for your Negative Thoughts

_____

_____

Emotion _____

Examples: All-or-nothing thinking, overgeneralization, mental filter, disqualifying the positive, jumping to conclusions, Catastrophizing, Emotional Reasoning, Should Statements, Mislabeling, Personalization.
Web search them to learn more about them

6. Adaptive response
What is a more balanced, realistic or objective way of seeing the situation?

_____

_____

_____

Emotion _____

7. Rerate feelings and emotions (0 - 100%)

Rerate your Beliefs about your Thoughts and Feelings. Add new Thoughts or emotions too

_____

_____

_____

Emotion _____

🌿 *Self-Worksheet 14:*
ReShaping™ My Negative Thoughts 2

What is the Negative Thought?

_____

_____

_____

What evidence do I have to support this Negative Thought?

_____

_____

What evidence do I have to refute this Negative Thought?

_____

_____

What are the Feelings I have with this Thought?

_____

_____

If this Thought is true what will happen because of it?

_____

_____

What is a more balanced or alternative Thought?

_____

_____

Rerating my Feelings:

_____

_____

My ReShaping™ Plan:

_____

_____

 *Self-Worksheet 15:*
ReShaping™ My Negative Thoughts 3

Negative Thoughts control how we feel about our Selves and the world around us. Positive Thoughts lead to us feeling good and Negative Thoughts can put us down. Sometimes our Thoughts happen so quickly that we fail to notice them, but they can still affect our mood. These are called Automatic Thoughts.

Remember that our Automatic Thoughts are often negative and irrational. Identifying these Negative Automatic Thoughts (NATS) and replacing them with new Rational Thoughts can improve our mood.

Use the example Below to identify and ReShape™ the issue

Concern or Issue	Negative Thought	New Thought
EXAMPLE: I made a mistake at work	"I'm probably going to be fired. I always mess up. This is it. I'm really bad at this job."	"I messed up, but mistakes happen. I'm going to work through this, like I always do."

CHAPTER 13

On Willingly ReShaping™ My Feelings Knowing They Become My Words

ur Feelings are, in fact, Emotional Thoughts causing our Emotional (Over) Reactions. Our Emotional (Over)-Reactions are usually caused by our Thoughts; however, sometimes our brain can also activate an Emotional (Over)-Reaction unconsciously (meaning that we may not understand why that Emotional (Over)-Reaction is happening).

Our Emotional (Over)-Reactions to these Emotional Thoughts (Feelings) involve changes in (1) what our bodies are doing, (2) what we pay attention to and think about, and (3) how we want to act.

After we have an Emotional (Over)-Reaction, it is important to pay attention to the underlying Feeling and to try our best to figure out which Emotions we are actually Feeling and why. Finally, researchers have revealed that it is important to know how our Emotions work because this can help us respond to our (Over)-Reactive Feelings in healthier ways.

Research has also found that certain kinds of Thoughts often lead to certain Emotions. For example, when a Womin™ thinks, "I'm in danger," she will more than likely feel Fear.

Or, when someone thinks, "I just lost someone I care about," that she will unquestionably feel Sad (or sometimes Anger). Or, when she thinks, "I just got what I wanted," that person will undoubtedly feel Happy.

Lastly, when she thinks, "That man just treated me unjustly," then she will probably feel angry.

183

It has also been revealed that the Thoughts that cause our Emotions usually answer questions like the ones below:

> *(1) Is what has happened unexpected?*
>
> *(2) Is what has happened enjoyable?*
>
> *(3) Is what has happened my fault or is it someone else's?*
>
> *(4) Can I control what happens next?*
>
> *(5) Will I be able to manage with what happened?*
>
> *(6) Does what has happened match with what I believe to be right or wrong?*
>
> *(7) Is what has happened going to make it easier or harder for me to get what I want?*

When something happens, we feel different emotions, depending on how our mind answers these different questions. But we can also Feel an Emotion (get feelings) and not know why sometimes. Remember that we Wimmin™ can feel Emotions even though they haven't noticed any Thoughts connected to those Emotions.

While this can be hard to understand, it has been found that at times our brains can unconsciously activate our Emotions.

This simply means that our brains might (unconsciously) notice something in our situation and activate an Emotional (Over)-Reaction, all without our even noticing it. In fact, it has been found that our brains do lots of things that we don't notice.

These are called "Unconscious Processes". This means that, even though we don't notice it, our brain is controlling many things in our body right now, such as our heart's beating.

The next time you're feeling an Emotional (Over)-Reaction and can't see the underlying Thought, try to pay a bit more attention as to what's happening in your current situation; or review the seven questions discussed earlier; or complete the "Self-Worksheet" exercise, which follows; this might help you figure out why you are "having Feelings".

May you be Blessed to live Maatfully™ every day . . .

Self-Worksheet 16:
On Events Thoughts & Feelings

Think of a time when something happened in your own life that led you to Feeling down [depressed] or unsettled [anxious].

What Thoughts and Emotions went through your mind? Use the example below to better clarify and determine your underlying Thoughts and Emotions:

EXAMPLE

EVENT:
Imani didn't get the promotion she'd expected she'd get.

THOUGHT(S):
What if I'm not as good at my job as I think I am? What if they're planning on firing me instead?

EMOTION(S):
Anxious

EXERCISE

EVENT): _____

_____

THOUGHT(S): _____

_____

EMOTION(S): _____

_____

CHAPTER 14

On Willingly ReShaping™ My Words Knowing They Become My Actions

What Are Emotive Words?

Over the years I've found that many of my clients have very little control over their emotive words. Words are the text of a story; or lyrics of a song, as opposed to the music; they are angry speech (esp. in the phrase, "to have words with someone"); or in to "eat one's words", as in, retracting what you've previously said.

Expressing our feelings with words is one of the many ways in which we engage our Selves with our words. Another is in actively keeping a variety of personal journals, where we use emotive words to "free writing" using a pen and notepad to define, identify and express our emotional Thoughts.

What Is Rumination?
In psychology, the term refers to obsessive repetition of Thoughts, words of feeling and excessively thinking about problems without solving the problem.

Rumination is habitually becoming preoccupied with something and not being able to get it out of our mind; as well it is a planned strategy of trying to control our upsetting problems. It's also repeatedly thinking about events from our past; dwelling on difficulties and things which distress us.

Is Rumination (Repetitive Emotional Words) Normal?
Although rumination is normal, excessive rumination can become problematic. Most of the time, and for most people, rumination is time-limited: it stops when the problem

is solved. To some extent everyone ruminates or dwells on their problems. Thinking about our problems can be helpful, especially if we reach a solution and put it into action

Here's a Few Ways in Which Rumination Are Excessive:

• *Unhelpful rumination can lead to inactivity and avoidance of problem-solving.*

• *Rumination tends to focus on what has gone wrong and can lead to negative thinking.*

• *Unhelpful rumination tends to focus on causes and consequences instead of solutions:*

    • *When used excessively, rumination can lead to depression.*

    • *When used excessively, rumination can maintain an episode of depression.*

    • *"What did I do to deserve this" and "Will my life ever get better?", instead of "How can I make my life better?".*

May you be Blessed to live Maatfully™ every day . . .

Self-Worksheet 17: Reducing Chronic Worry and Rumination

Reframe most Thoughts as "cerebral noise" or "mind junk" rather than important data that must be examined carefully. Distinguish "good" and "bad" worry whenever possible. Don't be your own worst enemy by indulging your Self in worries and by rationalizing your continuing to do so as if you could think your way to feeling better.

Learn to accept the presence of a worried Thought without having to take it so seriously and without having to get rid of it. How do you (overtly and covertly) value and seek worry?

How do you worry about worry and (overtly and covertly) try to avoid it? In other words, how do you get locked into a vicious circle of (overt and covert) approach and avoidance or reassurance-seeking?

Try using "scheduled worry" periods. Instead of indulging your worries by giving them your full attention whenever they intrude or by trying to avoid them, set up two or three 15-20 minute periods per day when you give your worries your complete attention.

When worries intrude at other times during the day, try to defer them to your next scheduled worry period. Seek Cognitive Therapy that focuses on common Cognitive Distortions that fuel worry. Learn diffusion skills to give your Self a degree of separation from recurrent worry content.

Examine Irrational Beliefs that often underpin worrying and rumination, such as:

> "The world should be fair and just."
> "I must be liked by everyone."
> "I cannot bear it when things are not as I would like them to be."
> "I can avoid trouble by worrying."
> "To be worthwhile, I must be thoroughly competent and exceptional."

189

Strive to relinquish the need for control and certainty. The search for both may seem irresistible and compelling at the moment, but, over time, it's entirely futile and only perpetuates worry and rumination.

Have a "do-able" Plan of Action (not the "right plan" or the "perfect plan") just a reasonable plan. Do you really have the facts? One can't escape one's own imagination, or run away from what "might" happen. Notice the mistakes you tolerate or excuse in others and then give your Self the same latitude. Do not rationalize your perfectionism as a Virtue.

Learn to take a mindful approach to moment-to-moment living: Stay in the "here-and-now" instead of "catastrophizing" about what could happen. (Try focusing on your senses, your actions, and your surroundings in the present moment).

Ask your Self these questions when you're stuck in a non-stop rumination, worry mode:

 "Am I overestimating the risk the way I typically do?"
 "What's the evidence?"
 "Am I trying to answer unanswerable questions?"
 "Am I trying to control things that I can't possibly control?"

CHAPTER 15

On Willingly ReShaping™ My Actions Knowing They Become My Habits

fter you've learned to manage any over-thinking about emotional words, which often keep you from meaningful taking action to change a disturbing problem or situation, you want to focus on managing your over-reactions.

ROLE OF FEAR IN DARING TO TAKE ACTION

According to the research, there are four main fears which negatively affect us: fear of judgement, fear of failure, fear of death, and fear of public speaking.

To make Optimism effective in bringing change in our life, we need to "take Action". But "Taking Action" can feel threatening and scary because it stirs up all our fears and anxieties of what that change might bring.

Fear cripples us. It keeps us stuck and paralyzed from moving forward. And it causes so many people to give up on whatever they're pursuing.

Taking action in the face of fear can feel impossible. It's sort of like driving in reverse while looking ahead. But, it doesn't have to be that way.

As J. Canfield has said, "Everything you want in life is on the other side of fear." So, what should you do then?

You will learn that the key to releasing fears and anxieties is by first becoming self-aware of them and then consciously recognizing that they no longer help or serve your present reality. This is the Way to obtaining the 1ˢᵗ level toward lasting SistahPeace™

As you move forward and complete the next Self Worksheet; you will start to proactively ReShape™ this process which will also learn to ReShape™ our unwanted unconscious habits and patterns.

Practice employing G. Litchfield's technique to one of your worries right now:

Question No. 1 -What am I worrying about? (Please write your answer to that question in the space below.)

_____

_____

Question No. 2 -What can I do about it? (Please write your answer to that question in the space below.)

_____

_____

Question No. 3 -Here is what I am going to do about it.

_____

_____

Question No. 4 -When am I going to start doing it?

Get the facts. Remember that D. Hawkes of Columbia University said that, "half the worry in the world is caused by people trying to make decisions before they have sufficient knowledge on which to base a decision."

After carefully weighing all the facts, come to a decision.

Once a decision is carefully reached, act on it! Get busy carrying out your decision- and dismiss any anxiety about the outcome.

When you are tempted to worry about a problem, write out and answer the following questions:

A. What is the problem?

_____

B. What is the cause of the problem?

_____

_____

C. What are all possible solutions?

_____

_____

D. What is the best solution?

_____

_____

Remember the old adage:
        "Actions speak louder than words . . ."

May you be Blessed to live Maatfully™ every day . . .

Self-Worksheet 18:
My Short-Term Goals
And Plan of Action

MY SHORT-TERM GOALS ARE:

1 _____

_____

2. _____

_____

3 _____

_____

4 _____

_____

5. _____

_____

STEPS I CAN TAKE TO ACCOMPLISH MY SHORT-TERM GOALS ARE (PLAN OF ACTION):

_____

_____

_____

_____

_____

_____

CHAPTER 16

Willingly ReShaping™ My Habits Knowing They Become My Patterns

hat Exactly Are Good Habits?

Psychology Today notes that, "Habit formation is the process by which behaviors become automatic. Habits can form without a person intending to acquire them, but they can also be deliberately Kultivated™—or eliminated—to better suit one's personal goals."

Habit Formation: Resolve, Rehearse, Repeat

Changing habits can seem difficult, especially when you're trying to adopt a new habitual behavior. A formidable array of psychological ideas are at the root formation of a new habit.

- **Resolve** firmly that you will pursue this new habit.
- **Rehearse** this new habit to set your Self up for success.
- **Repeat** this new habit enough times to make it automatic.

Around 2010, P. Lally, revealed that it actually takes anywhere from 18 to 254 days for a new habit to take hold, depending on how difficult and complex it was. The typical habit took 6 days to set it Self anew.

A simple new routine such as drinking a glass of water after breakfast can become automatic in about 20 days, yet a more complex process, like doing sit-ups after breakfast every day, could take a couple of months.

So, as we strive to kultivate™ a new habit, pause to consider the degree of difficulty of the new habit, exactly how motivated we are to formulate it, and our ability to execute it.

Then informally rank it on a scale ranging from regular water-drinking (20 days) to establishing a meditation daily (150 days) to estimate how long it will take to successfully make it habitual. Double that number, just to be on the safe side. Resolve to repeat this new habit or pattern for that number of days, and the odds are good we'll effectively establish as a solid habit.

Fortunately, these concepts and practices bundle nicely into an easy-to-remember trio of familiar actions. If we want to make a behavior a habit, remember to regularly do this with a specific habit:

And if we find our healthy habits still aren't going according to plan, we can try the following:

Stacking our habits: *Try introducing a habit by taking advantage of an existing habit to cue the new behavior. For example, if we have to take medication, we could put it next to our toothbrush, or next to our coffee maker so that we get the automatic cue each morning, "I brush my teeth, I take my meds," or "I make my coffee, I take my meds." This can be more successful than relying on recall, memory, and willpower.*

Swapping our habits: *Try taking a habit that we already have, and replace it with something similar but more aligned with our goals. For example, if we want to avoid sugary sodas, we could buy bottled water instead. The packaging is the similar, we buy from the same place, and we carry and use it the same way. Because we already have a habit, it will be easy to swap one product for another and also improve our health.*

The beginning of any new situation is typically a great time to create new goals. But if we also create a habit to help achieve our goal, our newly created habit is more likely to stick.

For example, let's say, we work really hard to lose 15 pounds, but if we don't decide to make "dieting and exercising" a lasting habit, it's likely we gain back that weight. Creating habits to achieve a goal can be hard at times, but it doesn't need to be!

Here are four workable approaches to developing new, lasting habits to help us achieve and keep our goals.

1: Make It Simple - The first mistake we might make when trying to develop a new habit is thinking we can rely too much on our willpower. Sometimes we're really motivated, and other days we just want to sit on the couch. Our motivation could change depending on our mood, the weather, and any number of other factors.

One way to help overcome the unpredictability of our levels of motivation is to break down a habit into more manageable parts so it requires less motivation to complete.

For example, say you want to start reading each night before bed. Instead of trying to read for 30 minutes, start with a goal of 5 minutes. When our motivation is low we can keep our momentum by getting through just 10 minutes of reading, increasing it as we feel we wish to, on any given night.

To help increase our willpower, we can try the "LifeCare" strategy of using WOOP—Wish, Outcome, Obstacle, Plan—strategy, which could help us generate the energy and motivation to help us achieve our goals.

Step 1: Wish
WOOP begins by setting a meaningful goal or "wish." Think about something in our lives we want to work toward: our career, schoolwork, relationships, or anything personal. It should be challenging, realistic, and attainable.

Steps 2 and 3: Outcome and Obstacle
Now that we have set your goal, the next 2 steps will help us generate the energy we need to get you moving toward your goal.

Sub Step 2: Outcome:
Think about what it would look and feel like to have our goal fulfilled. Take some time to deeply imagine, see, and feel what it would be like to attain the best possible outcome.

Sub Step 3 Obstacle:
Just thinking positively about the best outcome isn't enough, though, because there are obstacles that inevitably get in the way of our goals. Imagine an obstacle that we can control from within, such as Thoughts, feelings, bad habits, or actions—that might prevent us from working toward our goal.

Take some time to deeply imagine what it might feel like to encounter that obstacle. Steps 2 and 3 together help get us motivated. Fantasizing about the outcome gets us excited about our goal.

This positive thinking might help us feel good, and it might be enough to get us to do the "easy things". However, it's not enough to generate the motivation we need to buck up and do the hard stuff. This is why we need to contrast our positive thinking with the reality of the obstacles standing in our way. Steps 2 and 3 together can provide us with the motivation to do what's needed to accomplish our goal.

Imagine you're the captain of a football team trying to motivate our Selves and teammates to win the Super Bowl. We would want to envision the glory we would all feel holding the trophy at the end of the game, but that alone won't get us motivated to do all the work needed to win.

We would also need to focus on what's standing in the way of that glory: our opponent, our obstacle, our enemy! Now our team is fired up and motivated to do whatever it takes, but being energized and motivated alone isn't enough. We need a plan to overcome our obstacles so we can win the Super Bowl.

Sub Step 4: Plan
Finally, devise a plan to overcome the obstacles we've identified. This plan involves "when...then" statements known as "implementation intentions."

We might think, "WHEN (obstacle), THEN I will (effective plan)."

Repeat this for each obstacle we've identified. Using "when...then" statements helps us deliberately connect our plan to the obstacles we have identified ahead of time.

For example, the obstacle to our goal to run a 5K might be that we tend to sit on the couch and watch TV when we get home from work instead of going for a run.

We could devise the plan of
"WHEN coming home from work,
THEN immediately change into running clothes and go for a run. "

202

The WHEN...THEN strategy prevents us from wasting mental energy deciding what we should do because we already have an automatic plan in place.

2: Set Up Our Environment for Success

Another way to help create a new habit is to set up our environment so that it's easier to do the things we want to do and harder to do the things that gets in our way.

For example, if one of the main obstacles to reading each night before bed is that we're tempted to use social media apps on our phone instead, try putting those apps in folders so it takes more effort to open them.

Even better, charge our phone out of arm's reach of our bed or even in another room if possible. Place the book we want to read on your nightstand so it takes little effort to begin reading. This helps make our new habit the easiest thing for us to do each night.

3: Build On Routines We Already Have

Another part of starting a new habit is remembering to do it. This might seem easy, but as the stresses of life build up it can become hard to remember to do our new "habit". Setting alarms or putting up sticky-note reminders can be effective, but it's even easier if we link the new habit to a routine we already do; and we won't clutter our house with sticky notes everywhere!

For example, if we want to be more grateful, each night at dinner ask each person at the table to share 3 things she is grateful for. If we want to lose weight, do 15 squats after each time we brush our teeth. When creating a new habit, think of routines that we already do as often as the new habit we want to create, and then link them together.

4: Embrace Failure and Enjoy the Process

If we can't get our Selves to do the new "habit" at first, don't lose hope! It can be frustrating, but developing habits is often a "trial-and error" process. If we don't succeed at first, we can just switch things up. Learn from those errors: If one thing doesn't work, just try something else.

Maybe, as described above, we can break down the habit to make it simpler or find a different routine to connect it to. And try to enjoy the process! If our desired habit is to

203

eat cookies every day, it's likely we'll succeed in no time, because eating cookies is fun. Find a way to make every new habit fun: Congratulate our Selves after each success instead of beating our Selves up after each failure.

To summarize ~ creating new habits is a great way to set our Selves up for long-term success in accomplishing new goals. Try these four strategies;

1. Making the habit simple.
2. Setting up our environment for success.
3. Building on current routines.
4. Finding ways to enjoy the process; which can help us make any process easier and more fun.

Sistahs, Here's A Few Good Thoughts to Consider:

The positive results of adopting small, healthier habits may be imperceptible at first, but they compound quickly when replacing bad behaviors.

"But when we repeat 1 percent errors, day after day, by replicating poor decisions, duplicating tiny mistakes, and rationalizing little excuses, our small choices compound into toxic results", writes author J. Clear.

Regularly Consider The Following:

➤Conscious Choice simply means we're Willing because we've become Proactively Aware.

➤Have an awareness that an Attitude is merely choosing how we think about our Thoughts.

➤We can SheChange™ our Attitude by SheChanging™ what we think about our Thoughts and Beliefs.

➤Fearfulness is generated by our Negative Expectations and beliefs about our being Inadequate.

➤Anxiety is Fearfulness, which is our scaring our Selves by believing our Negative Uncertain Expectations.

➤Awareness is not Knowing, because Knowing is Proactive Awareness Befriending Confident Expectations.

➢Denial is an Active Refusal to Acknowledge.

➢Willingness is, an Active Unawareness of, yet agreeing to reconsider to become Aware and Trusting of the Potential enough to decide to SheChange™.

➢Knowing is Active Acknowledgement.

➢Stress is anger about fears of victimization (Feeling) inadequate about a [pending] outcome.

➢Worry is feeling stuck, and is an intense need to try to control things.

➢Ingrained is habitually believing something can't be changed.

➢Non-judgement and quiet creates a SistahPeaceful™ Mindset.

➢Still waters DO run deep – so sometimes, simply Be Still.

May you be Blessed to live Maatfully™ every day . . .

❧Self-Worksheet 19:
SheChanging™ Our Attitude
by SheChanging™ Our Habits

How do we keep a positive attitude when we're discouraged and frustrated? What if some days we have a bunch of problems piling up after another? What if our work environment is negative? Is it possible to see life differently?

We have mind-sets that filter information. Each of us has attitudes or beliefs about people places and events, and these attitudes decide which of our perceptions we'll allow our brains to interpret, believe and what we will filter out. Meaning that our attitudes have a lot to do with how we perceive and relate to others, to the world, and even how we actually see our Selves.

Most of us essentially resist SheChange™. Even when we're aware of a bad habit, it's sometimes difficult to SheChange™ it. However, our ability to adapt to new situations is not only important, but often crucial to success in our desired goals.

Create Proactive SheChange™ Plan:
Below are four simple steps for proactively SheChanging™ of one habit at a time (Oliveira, 2015):

1) *Choose one keystone habit and do it well. It is ideal to select one goal that will bring your life in line. Be sure to the habit easy and then slowly enhance the degree of difficulty.*

2) *Write down your plan: Try to create a habit loop: cue, routine and reward. Make visible what you will do each day. Remember to start off slow, focusing on creating ritual first and results second. Also, define success in measurable terms.*

3) *Make your goal public and develop a support team: Ask your family, friends or colleagues to help hold you accountable. Be sure to report your progress each day, either within a journal or through your favorite social media outlet.*

4) *Make a plan for when you falter. Write down what caused you to stumble. You want to be as honest as possible. Most importantly, don't be afraid to start over*

207

with a revised plan.

When a professional staffing service asked over 1,000 executives, to rank the characteristics that they saw as essential for an employee to succeed, they listed among them; "Adapts easily to change" and "Motivated to learn new skills", ranked #1 and #2. Surveys like this have spurred companies to hold employee seminars on the importance of adapting to SheChange™ and growing professionally along with the company.

Surprisingly, "Creating Positive SheChange™ Habits" are learned; and can be unlearned. Adopting new habits requires an earnest desire to change, consistent effort, time, and commitment.

Try the following strategies for eliminating old habits and acquiring positive new ones.

1. Be willing to SheChange™. *As with all learning, we must desire and see the value and meaning in developing a positive attitude and habits. It's easy to find excuses. At some point, we must be willing to find reasons to actually SheChange™.*

It further helps to identify specific goals: "I really want to be more optimistic and to get along with people easier," "I'm determined to see problems and find creative alternatives," "I have control over my Thoughts and behavior." Remember that lasting change requires desire, effort, and commitment.

2. Focus on the positive. *Are you a glass-half-empty or glass-half-full type of person? Practice being able seeing the good qualities in our Selves, and in others as well as the positive side of any situation.*

Dispute our negative Thoughts and beliefs with critical thinking and use creative problem solving to explore the best outcomes; for example, "I missed our work-study meeting. I'll email my test questions to the group, apologize, and offer to do extra assignments. This mix-up has reminded me just how important it is to check the calendar each morning."

3. Develop specific goals. *Setting specific goals is an effective beginning for change. Statements such as, "I wish I could get better reviews" and "I hope I can stop being bored so often." are too general and only help us continue our bad habits.*

Goals such as, "I will exercise for 30 minutes, once a day." is specific and can be

208

assessed and measured for achievement.

4. Only change one habit at a time. *We'll likely become discouraged when trying to change too many things about our Selves at the same time.*

If we have decided to exercise for 30 minutes, once a day, in our home, and then do this for a month, then two months, and so on will it become a firm habit. Only after we've made one successful change, should we move on to the next.

5. Start small. *Appreciate that consistently taking small steps each day will produce major results. Sometimes the smallest changes can make the biggest difference.*

For example, don't put off starting an exercise program because we don't have time for a long workout. Just start small by walking to class instead of driving or taking a walk at lunch.

6. Use affirmations to imagine success. *Imagine your Self progressing through all the steps toward your desired goal.*

For example, we see our Selves sitting on our couch in our comfortable living room. Calmly affirm, "I am calm and find it easy to concentrate. I enjoy writing and feel good about completing my work projects." Or before you get out of your bed in the morning, pause to imagine your day effortlessly unfolding: "I'm positive, calm and focused . . . and I'll easily accomplish everything on my to-do list".

7. Be aware of your Thoughts and Behaviors. *Pay attention to your behavior and reflect on ways you can be more successful. For example, you may notice that the schoolwork you complete late at night is not as thorough as the work you complete earlier in the day.*

Taking due notice when we feel less stressed or when you take 10 minutes at night to review our day, or when we lay out clothes; and pre-review for the next day's events.

8. Be more patient and persistent. *Remind our Selves that lasting change requires a pattern of consistent behavior. By our remembering to be patience with our process, the changes will eventually begin to feel comfortable and normal.*

Remember that we can't let our Selves become discouraged and give up, when we haven't seen a complete SheChange™ in our behavior in a few weeks.

Give your Self at least a month of progress toward our goal. If we fall short one day, get back on track the next. Lasting SheChange™ requires time, be patient with our expectations.

Make a Commitment and Learn to Apply Positive Habits

Committing to good habits is the foundation for reinforcing the cycle of success. Read the following statements concerning habits for success that we have discussed in this text.

Write either Yes or No as each statement applies to you.

Can you create a motivated, resourceful state of mind? _____

Do you know how to solve problems creatively? _____

Do you use critical thinking in making decisions? _____

Do you exercise daily? _____

Do you maintain your ideal weight? _____

Do you keep your body free of harmful substances and addictions? _____

Do you support your body by eating healthy foods? _____

Do you practice techniques for managing your stress? _____

Have you developed an effective budget? _____

Do you take time for career planning? _____

If you find you've answered "No" to many of these questions, don't be alarmed. When old habits are too ingrained, it's difficult to change them.

Select at least one of the habits you answered No to. Determine what you can do today to turn it into a positive habit.

Self-Worksheet 20:
Am I Ready to SheChange™ & Improve My Life Now?

[Please check the topics that will most SheInspire™ you to improve your life.]

	I want to work on this now	I will do this at a later time	Not something I want to work on now
1. I now have the opportunity to do something I've always wanted to do.	_____	_____	_____
2. What have I always wanted to do?			

_____
_____

3. I now have the opportunity to discover what type of life I'd really love to have.	_____	_____	_____
4. I'd like to explore what will make me happy in my life.	_____	_____	_____
5. I can now explore those choices that are more aligned with values and interests. What are my values and interests?	_____	_____	_____

_____
_____

6. I'd like to work on my interviewing skills and the way I present myself.	_____	_____	_____
7. I'd like to work on my job hunting skills.	_____	_____	_____
8. I want to work on my résumé so that it presents me in the best possible light.	_____	_____	_____

211

	I want to work on this now	I will do this at a later time	Not something I want to work on now

9. *I'd like to go back to school to pursue additional training. What type of training?*   _____ _____ _____

_____

_____

10. *I'd like to go back to school and train for a completely different field.*   _____ _____ _____
What field?   _____ _____ _____

_____

_____

11. *I need some free time for myself right now.*   _____ _____ _____

12. *How will I enjoy this free time?*

_____

_____

13. *I've been out of balance for a while and I need to get back in balance.*
What's out of balance?

_____

_____

14. *I've been avoiding some things in my life and now is the time to take care of some things.*   _____ _____ _____

What are these things?

_____

_____

15. *I'm not the person I used to be and I need to*   _____ _____ _____
explore the person I am today. Who did I used to be?

_____

	I want to work on this now	I will do this at a later time	Not something I want to work on now

Who am I now?

_____

_____

16. *I have the opportunity to learn from my mistakes and things that didn't go well.*   _____   _____   _____

What were the mistakes I've chosen not to make again?

_____

_____

What have I learned for the future?

_____

_____

17. *It's important for me to explore why I sell my Self short and settle for less than I really want.*   _____   _____   _____

How do I sell my Self short?

_____

_____

18. *I've allowed my fears to stop me before and now I need to move past them.*   _____   _____   _____

What fears have stopped me in the past?

_____

_____

19. *I've sabotaged my Self or held my Self back from success and now I am willing and emotionally ready to be successful.*   _____   _____   _____
How did I hold my Self back?

213

	I want to work on this now	I will do this at a later time	Not something I want to work on now

20. I need to ask and allow for more help and support to come from others.   _____   _____   _____

21. It's important for me to get more comfortable talking with and networking with strangers.   _____   _____   _____

22. I'd like to focus more on my spiritual life.   _____   _____   _____

How_____

_____

23. I'd like to put more focus on my family life. How?   _____   _____   _____

_____

_____

24. I have the opportunity to improve my relationships with others.   _____   _____   _____

_____

_____

_____

_____

_____

_____

CHAPTER 17

On Willingly ReShaping™ My Patterns Knowing They Become My Beliefs

ur patterns are propelled by our Thoughts and emotions. Let's say you want to lose weight but you keep eating sweets in the break room. The choice to eat the tasty snack is based on your Thoughts and Emotions. Your hand does not reach into the bowl on its own accord. It does not have its own brain which makes it move without your permission.

You might have a core belief that contradicts to your goal. By design, core beliefs are held in the subconscious mind just outside of conscious awareness. They act as blueprint instructions determining your choices.

We might have a goal to advance our career. But because of several childhood learning problems, we're under the belief that we're not smart enough to be successful in our goal. This negative belief subconsciously predominates any desires to realize our dreams.

So, while we may find we're doing good initially, much too soon we start to believe the growing seeds of doubt take over and we start to tell our Selves really negative comments like "this is just too hard and not worth the effort". Subconsciously we've already decided we'll only fail, so we eventually just, "say it into being".

Given these negative patterns of beliefs appear to be created out of our conscious awareness most of us never bother to examine them. Consequently, every time we unknowingly repeat them, we strengthen them. This is how our subconscious habits are hardened into our subconscious patterns.

In order to change our subconscious patterns, it's useful to understand two basic rules of humin™ behavior:

1. There is a positive intention motivating all behaviors.
2. The subconscious mind will go to any length to protect you and what you believe to be true (even if it's actually Self-defeating).

Kultural™ Roots of Our Patterns

Our Kultural™ patterns are shared beliefs, values, norms, and social practices that are stable over time and that lead to roughly similar behaviors across similar situations.

Language, symbols, values, and traditional "norms" are among the more important elements of Kultural™. Our religious beliefs, customs and traditions, art, as well as history, put together are considered as the Kultural™ elements of a group.

According to Google sites, there are four components of Kultural™ patterns.

A belief is an idea that we assume to be true about the world. Beliefs, therefore, are a set of learned interpretations that form the basis for Kultural™ members to decide what is and what is not logical and permissible.

Values involve what a Kultural™ group regards as good or bad, right or wrong, fair or unfair, just or unjust, beautiful or ugly, clean or dirty, valuable or worthless, appropriate or inappropriate.

Because values are the desired characteristics or goals of a Kultural™, a Kulture's™ values do not necessarily describe its actual behaviors and characteristics. However, values are often offered as the rationalization for the way in which its members communicate.

Norms are the socially shared expectations of what's appropriate behavior. When a Womin's™ behaviors violate the appropriate Kultural™ norms, social sanctions are usually imposed. Similar to values, norms can vary within a Kulture™ in terms of their importance and intensity. Unlike values, however, norms often change over a period of time, whereas beliefs and values tend to be much more durable.

Social practices are merely the predictable behavior patterns that members of a

Kulture™ typically follow. Meaning that our social patterns and practices are the outward manifestation of beliefs, values, and norms.

One view of Kultural™ patterns contains five major elements that address the manner in which a Kulture™ orients itself to activities, social relations, the Self, the world, and the passage of time.

- *Activity orientation: how the members of a Kultural™ view humin™ actions and the expression of Self through activities.*

- *Social relations orientation: designates how members in a Kulture™ organize themselves and relate to one another.*

- *Self-orientation describes how member's identities are formed, whether the Kultural™ views the Self as changeable, what motivates individual actions, and the kind of members who're valued and respected.*

- *Kultural™ patterns also tell members how to locate themselves in relation to the spiritual, AnSistahral™ world, nature, and other living things.*

- *Time orientation: how people conceptualize time. Time orientation provides answers to questions such as the following:*

    - *How should time be valued and understood?*

    - *Is time a scarce resource, or is it unlimited?*

    - *Is the desirable pace of life fast or slow?*

    - *Is time linear or cyclical?*

Given the above, lasting SheChange™ of our patterns may seem hard (to us) because it's like trying to climb up a very tall peak, with only the anticipation of uncertainty on the other side. Rather than focusing on huge, transformational SheChange™, effort to conquer smaller, incremental SheChanges™. Instead of taking a leap, make a (more doable) step.

Making an initial move (and seeing success from it) has a major impact on our brains. A 2009 study revealed that we absorb more lessons from success than we do from failure. It also found that each subsequent success is incrementally processed more efficiently by us.

In short, our brains learn pretty fast what makes us succeed, so we can repeat it. If we want to create lasting behavioral patterns of SheChange™, we can decide to lose the all or nothing mentality. We can be willing to put our Selves out there, even if it's one small SheChange™ at a time.

May you be Blessed to live Maatfully™ every day . . .

Self-Worksheet 21:
Making Life-Long SheChange™

Part 1: Exploring the SheChange™

1. *What life pattern / habit has been difficult for me to SheChange™?*

_____

_____

2. *What is the benefit of SheChanging™ this pattern / habit?*

_____

_____

3. *What do I get from maintaining this pattern / habit?*

_____

_____

4. *What will I lose by SheChanging™ this pattern / habit?*

_____

_____

5. *What is it costing me to __not__ make this SheChange™?*

_____

_____

6. *On a scale of 1 – 10, how committed am I to SheChanging™ this pattern / habit?*
(10 is highest)

_____

_____

7.What action steps could I take this month to SheChanging™ this pattern /

_____

_____

Part 2: Rooting Into Past Success

8.What is one positive SheChange™ that I have made in my life?

_____

_____

9.How did I go about making that SheChange™?

_____

_____

10.How could I bring that same energy / perspective into my life right now?

_____

_____

CHAPTER 18

On Willingly ReShaping™ My Beliefs Knowing They Become My Character

Core beliefs is the common clinical term for what I call positive and negative Character labels.
~ Alice Boyles

 hat Are Our Core Beliefs?

Core beliefs are a Womin's™ most fundamental guiding principles or attitudes. These guiding principles dictate behavior and can help Wimmin™ understand the difference between right and wrong.

Core beliefs are a Womin's™ most central ideas about them Selves, others, and the world. These beliefs act like a lens through which every situation and life experience is seen.

Because of this, Wimmin™ with different core beliefs might be in the same situation, but think, feel, and behave very differently.

Even if a core belief is inaccurate, it still shapes how a Womin™ sees the world. Harmful core beliefs lead to negative Thoughts, feelings, and behaviors, whereas rational core beliefs lead to balanced reactions.

Nothing seems more urgent than working on our core beliefs when they are preventing us from flourishing in our lives. They are the root cause of most of our psychological problems, determining our Self-perceptions, cognitions, beliefs about the world and others, and personal rules. They also generate and shape our Negative Automatic Thoughts.

223

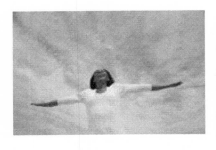

Cognitive restructuring techniques are often used to train our minds to embrace more productive attitudes. We can venture to unearth the origins of habits and patterns in our experiences and use our interpretations as guides for uncovering their all-pervasive influence.

We can also manage them by using positive psychology approaches, such as ACT-based interventions. These approaches seek to shift our focus away from problematic cognitions to kultivating™ value, meaning, and taking positive action. Rather than trying to correct negative core beliefs, they simply suggest that we accept them and be mindful of the fact that they are little more than mere opinions.

Common Harmful Core Beliefs

However, harmful core beliefs are very difficult to control and eradicate and have the power to cause long-term damage. Core beliefs are often hidden beneath surface-level beliefs.

For example, the core belief "no one likes me" might underlie the surface belief "my friends only spend time with me out of pity".

Helpless
"I am weak"
"I am a loser"
"I am trapped"

Unlovable
"I am unlovable"
"I will end up alone"
"No one likes me"

Worthless
"I am bad"
"I don't deserve to live"
"I am worthless"

External Danger
"The world is dangerous"

224

"People can't be trusted"
"Nothing ever goes right"

Consequences of Harmful Core Beliefs
Interpersonal Problems
❖*difficulty trusting others*
❖*feelings of inadequacy in relationships*
❖*excessive jealousy*
❖*overly confrontational or aggressive*
❖*putting others' needs above one's own needs*

Mental Health Problems
❖*Depression*
❖*Anxiety*
❖*substance abuse*
❖*difficulty handling stress*
❖*low self-esteem*

Facts About Core Beliefs
1. People are not born with core beliefs—they are actually learned.
2. Core beliefs usually develop in childhood, or during stressful or traumatic periods in adulthood.
3. Information that contradicts core beliefs is often ignored.
4. Negative core beliefs are not necessarily true, even if they feel true.
5. Core beliefs tend to be rigid and long-standing. However, they can be SheChanged™.

Learn and regularly practice letting go of outdated self-sabotaging core beliefs and proactively replacing them. Use the following Self Worksheets to help you further.

May you be Blessed to live Maatfully™ every day . . .

Self-Worksheet 22:
Our Core Beliefs

Core beliefs are a Womin's™ most central ideas about her Self, others, and the world. These beliefs act like a lens, through which every situation and life experience is seen.

Core beliefs are our most deeply held assumptions about ourselves, the world, and others. They are firmly embedded in our thinking, and significantly shape our reality and behaviors. Yet, as the name suggests, core beliefs are precisely that – beliefs rather than facts.

Based on our childhood valuations, they are often untrue. They are also Self-perpetuating. Like magnets, they attract false evidence that makes them stronger, and then they repel anything that might challenge them. But the good news is that it's always possible to SheChange™ them.

1. Please complete the statements below. Don't spend a long time thinking about them; simply write whatever comes into your head.

I am _____

_____

Other people are _____

_____

The world is _____

_____

2. Now think about the three statements. How do they make you feel? When did you first become aware of these beliefs? Which experiences fashioned them? Who in your life may hold similar views?

3. Ask your Self: Do these core beliefs still serve me? If not, which beliefs would be

227

more constructive? Write down three beliefs about your Self, other people, and the world which you would like to kultivate™ going forward:

I am _____

_____

Other people are _____

_____

The world is _____

_____

4. Whenever you become aware that the old core beliefs are coloring your thinking and interpretations of the world, recall their origins and how you see that they no longer serve you.

Try to remember your new core beliefs instead. How would you interpret an event or situation if you viewed it through the lens of your new beliefs?

_____

_____

_____

_____

_____

_____

_____

_____

_____

_____

_____

_____

_____

_____

_____

_____

Self-Worksheet 23:
Self-Reflections
About Our Core Values

The most important thing in the world to me is:

_____

I feel important when:

_____

_____

What is fun to me?

_____

_____

What is essential to me?

_____

_____

What do I need?

_____

_____

What can't I live without?

_____

What makes life worth living? Why do I get up in the morning?

_____

_____

CHAPTER 19

On Willingly ReShaping™ My Character Knowing It Becomes My Destiny . . .

Good Character is our Soul's Great Goal and it helps us to Actualize our Immortal Soul's Eternal Destiny Path.
~ AfraShe Asungi

I n our Mama Afrika traditions, values guide the behavior of every member. Specific mention could be made of values such as hospitality, truth, respect for old age, covenant keeping, hard work and good character. Stanford Encyclopedia of Philosophy, notes that:

> *"The character and conscience of a society is embedded in the ideas and beliefs about what is right or wrong, what is a good or bad character; it is also embedded in the conceptions of satisfactory social relations and attitudes held by the members of the society; it is embedded, furthermore, in the forms or patterns of behavior that are considered by the members of the society to bring about social harmony and cooperative living, justice, and fairness. The ideas and beliefs about moral conduct are articulated, analyzed, and interpreted by the moral thinkers of the society.*

> *African societies, as organized and functioning human communities, have undoubtedly evolved ethical systems—ethical values, principles, rules—intended to guide social and moral behavior. But, like African philosophy itself, the ideas and beliefs of the African society that bear on ethical conduct have not been given elaborate investigation and clarification and, thus, stand in real need of profound and extensive analysis and interpretation.*

233

In the last three decades or so, attempts have been made by contemporary African philosophers to give sustained reflective attention to African moral ideas. This entry is intended to make some contribution to the understanding of African ethical thinking.

The entry makes the Afrikan moral language its point of departure, for the language of morality gives insight into the moral thinking or ideas of the society. The centrality of the notions of character and moral personhood, which are inspired by the African moral language, is given a prominent place. The entry points up the social character of African ethics and highlights its affiliated notions of the ethics of duty (not of rights) and of the common good. The humanistic foundations and features of African ethics are extensively discussed."

The worth of a Womin's™ character all comes down to her core values and to her beliefs and motivations for acting as they do. In general, Wimmin™ who're considered to have good character often have traits like integrity, honesty, courage, loyalty, fortitude, and other important virtues that promote good behavior.

These character traits define who they are as people—and highly influence the choices they make in their lives. According to the research, one of the innovations of our Afrikan Social Truths are the sanctity of generous universal hospitality on which they [i.e., members of the community and others] could rely (J. Nyerere).

Most people, will testify, in amazement, to the principle of hospitality and generosity of continental Afrikans. This tenet is an expression of the timeless perception of our common huminity™ and our universal humin™ unity.

The Afrikan conception of the worth and dignity of the humin™ being, there is one Akan (Ghanaian) maxim that advises: "The humin™ being is more beautiful than gold." ("onipa ye fe sen sika")

In this maxim, a humin™ being is depicted as beautiful. And that which is "beautiful" is enjoyed for her own sake, not for the sake of anything else. What the maxim is saying, therefore, is that a humin™ being is to be enjoyed for her own sake. To enjoy a humin™ being for her own sake means we appreciate her value as a humin™ being and demonstrate that appreciation by showing compassion, generosity, and hospitality.

It means we should be open to the interests and welfare of others and feel it our moral duty to offer help where it is needed. To enjoy a humin™ being also means we recognize another person as an equivalent individual whose worth as a humin™ being is equal to ours; and with whom we share basic values, ideals, and sentiments.

Thus, the main intent of this maxim is to point out the worth of a humin™ being and the respect that is to be given to her by virtue of her huminity™. Recognition of the worth of a Sistah humin™ being, according to the maxim, is more important than kultivating™ wealth.

Furthermore, a WellBalanced™ Womin™ of good character does the right thing because she believes it is the right thing to do. She doesn't act because someone else is influencing or pressuring her to do so, and she doesn't do something merely because she wants to look good in front of others.

A "right action" life according

WellBalanced™ Womin™ takes because it is important to her to live to her personal values.

Character is thinkers in

earnestly defined by the Akan terms of habits, which result from a

Womin's™ deeds or actions: "character comes from your actions" (or deeds: "nneyee"), shares an Akan traditional thinker.

Tireless performance of a particular action will produce a undeniable habit and, thus, a corresponding character. To acquire virtue, a Womin™ has to perform good actions, that is, morally acceptable actions so that they become habitual.

The action or deed that led to the attainment of a newly good habit must be persistently performed in order to strengthen that habit; in this way, virtue (or, good character) is attained.

Over time such a practiced virtue becomes a habit. This is the position of Akan ethics on the development and attainment of a good (or, bad) character.

Character is, thus, a behavior pattern formed as a result of past persistent actions. Hence, moral virtues (excellences of character) or vices arise through habituation. This is also what the Akan mean when they say "aka ne ho", "it has remained with her," "it has become part of her," "it has become her habit."

235

Most of us believe that our unique qualities and traits are good—and while we may admit that there is room for improvement, we generally believe that we are living life about as well as we can.

However, if we're interested in further developing our character, it's important to understand which traits are markers of good character—and which traits are related to one another.

In general, most folk agree that values like honesty, integrity, loyalty, and dependability are good character traits to have. But of course, there are many other factors that are commonly found alongside these traits such as diligence, loyalty, responsibility, truthfulness, and more.

When we set a goal to have a certain character trait, we can more easily develop it by becoming more conscious of our actions—and by working to integrate appropriate behaviors into our daily lives.

Character Trait Examples

Character traits are valued aspects of a Womin's™ behavior. Everyone has character traits, both good and bad, including our favorite fictional characters.

Being a Womin™ of good character means she acts with honesty, respect, responsibility, caring, and other "good" traits.

A Womin™ of "good character" acts, thinks, and feels in a way that matches some commonly accepted "good" traits, like being honest, respectful, responsible, caring, fair.

The old expression that our actions speak louder than words is very true when it comes to character traits. We learn about a Womin's character by watching how she interacts with the world.

There's an endless array of character traits that can be used to describe your Self or others, we've provided a selection of positive character trait / Value examples here.

Some character traits show a Womin's™ underlying values or beliefs:
- *Generosity*
- *Integrity*

- *Loyalty*
- *Devotion*
- *Loving*
- *Kindness*
- *Sincerity*
- *Self-control*
- *Peacefulness*
- *Faithfulness*
- *Patience*
- *Determination*
- *Persistence*
- *Adventurous*
- *Fairness*
- *Cooperation*
- *Tolerance*
- *Optimism*
- *Spirituality*

6 Pillars of CHARACTER

Trustworthiness:

Worthy of Trust, Honor and Confidence Honesty: Trustful, Sincere, Candid, Non-deceptive, Non-cheating Integrity: Principled, Morally Courageous Promise Keeping: Reliable, Dependable.

- *Be honest in communications and actions.*
- *Don't deceive, cheat or steal.*
- *Be reliable, do what you say you'll do.*
- *Have the courage to do the right thing.*
- *Build a good reputation.*
- *Be loyal to your values.*
- *Keep your promises.*

Respect:

Regard for the Dignity, Worth and Autonomy of all People Conduct: With courtesy, civility and politeness in treating others.

- *Treat others with respect and follow the Golden Rule.*

- *Be accepting of differences.*
- *Use good manners, not bad language.*
- *Be considerate of the feelings of others.*
- *Don't threaten, hit or hurt anyone.*
- *Deal peacefully with anger, insults, and disagreements.*

Responsibility:

Acknowledgment and Performance of Duties, Accountability: Answerable for consequences of decisions Pursuit of Excellence: Diligence and Perseverance Self-Control: Doing the right thing and using moderation

- *Do what you are supposed to do.*
- *Plan ahead.*
- *Be diligent.*
- *Persevere.*
- *Do your best.*
- *Use self-control.*
- *Be self-disciplined.*
- *Think before you act.*
- *Be accountable for your words, actions and attitudes.*
- *Set a good example for others.*
- *Choose a positive attitude.*
- *Make healthy choices.*

Justice and Fairness:

Making Decisions on Appropriate Factors Impartiality: Avoidance of conflicts of interest Commitment to Equity and Equality: Reasonableness, consistency, due process and fair play, Openness: To information and the ideas of others

- *Play by the rules.*
- *Take turns and share.*
- *Be open-minded; listen to others.*
- *Don't take advantage of others.*
- *Don't blame others carelessly.*
- *Treat all people fairly.*

Caring:

Regard for the Well-Being of Others Consideration: Kindness, compassion,

unselfishness Charity: Altruism, Giving
- *Be kind.*
- *Be compassionate and show you care.*
- *Show empathy.*
- *Express gratitude.*
- *Forgive others and show mercy.*
- *Help people in need.*
- *Be charitable and altruistic.*

Civic Virtue and Citizenship:
Community Service Social Obligation: Recognizing and living up to the Civil Law: Following the rules and doing ones' share.
- *Do your share to make your home, school, community, and world better.*
- *Cooperate.*
- *Get involved in community affairs.*
- *Stay informed; vote.*
- *Be a good neighbor.*
- *Make choices that protect the safety and rights of others.*
- *Protect the environment.*
- *Volunteer.*

May you be Blessed to live Maatfully™ every day . . .

Self-Worksheet 24:
Self-Reflection: How's My Character

The question then, is, "What are the "good," or "positive," character traits, and how can we strengthen them, and what are "bad" ("negative") qualities and how can we minimize them?

Use these good character journal prompts to help you to gain a deeper awareness of the process of developing and maintaining positive character traits.

What character traits are most important to you? Why?

_____

_____

1. *What does it mean to you for someone to have good character? Write about someone you know who has it.*

_____

_____

2. *Write about a time when you had to give up something you really wanted for the sake of someone else.*

_____

_____

3. *Why do some Wimmin™ struggle so much with doing the right thing?*

_____

_____

241

4. *Do you think you have good character? Why or why not?*

_____

_____

5. *Write about a time when you struggled to make the right decision. How did you make a choice in the end?*

_____

_____

6. *What does it mean to have integrity?*

_____

_____

7. *Write about a time when you witnessed someone doing something kind that they didn't have to do. How did you respond?*

_____

_____

8. *What is the hardest lesson you've ever had to learn? Why?*

_____

_____

Self-Worksheet 25:
Which Parts Of My Self Now Want Expression?

What parts/ characteristics/ qualities would I like to express in my life?

Circle or put an X in front of those parts I'd like to more fully express.

Helper	*Friend*
Creative	*Organizer*
Family-Oriented Part	*Quiet Part*
Detail-Oriented Part	*Spiritual Part*
Fun Loving Part	*Writer*
Community-Oriented Part	*Teacher*
Analytic Side/ Thinker	*Loving Part*
Emotional Side	*Social Part*
Athletic/ Physical Part	*Mother / Father*
Talker/ Communicator	*Contemplative Part*
Artistic / Art-Lover	*Resourceful Part*
Other _____	*Other* _____

Self-Worksheet 26:
Core Life Values Self-Assessment

Please rate each value according to how important it is to you.

5 = Essential   4 = Very Important

3 = Somewhat Important   2 = Only Occasionally   1 = Not Important to Me

~.~.~.~.~.~.~.~.~.~.~.~.~.~.~~.~.~.~.~.~.~

_____ Independence

_____ Challenge

_____ Feeling Competent & Capable

_____ Peace and Tranquility

_____ Creative Expression

_____ Physical Activity

_____ Time Freedom

_____ Recognition and Acknowledgement

_____ Adventure

_____ Status

_____ Being involved community

_____ Simplicity

_____ Busy lifestyle

_____ Friendships

_____ Learning new things

_____ Accomplishment getting a lot done in my life

_____ Having a spiritual way of life

_____ Balanced lifestyle

_____ Living in accordance with high moral standards

_____ Change and variety

_____ Intimacy and closeness

_____ Social contact

_____ Having fun, engaging in leisure activities

_____ Contributing to society

_____ Stability and security

_____ Time with my immediate family

_____ Time with my extended family

_____ Time alone

_____ Pursuit of a hobby

_____ Healthy lifestyle

_____ Mental stimulation and growth as a person

_____ Psychological awareness

_____ Financial Freedom and/or abundance of money

_____ Successful management

_____ Taking on new projects

_____ Time in nature

~.~.~.~.~.~.~.~.~.~.~.~.~~.~.~.~.~.~

THE MOST IMPORTANT VALUES
I WANT TO FOCUS ON RIGHT NOW

[please take a moment to review the 7 highest numbered values from above, and include them by highest numbered value on this list.]

1. _____

2. _____

3. _____

4. _____

5. _____

6. _____

7. _____

CHAPTER 20

On Willingly ReShaping™ My Destiny . . .

Always Remember . . .
And Strive to Actively Affirm . . .
How Living with Purpose
Always Includes Mindfully Loving Your Self . . .
~ AfraShe Asungi

Many scholars describe destiny as , *"the greatest enigma is the puzzle of our ultimate destiny"*. Destiny is also defined as our future or the pre-ordained path of our lives, shaped by our actions and decisions, not by chance. ReShaping™ a New Thought Decides Our Life-Style / Our Destiny

We are the makers of our own destinies. Throughout the whole of this Workbook we've explained and guided our readers to recognize the importance of our Thoughts, feelings and (re)actions on our lives; on our outcomes, on our very destinies.

ReShape™ your quality of Life habits that start you on path of Self-Affirmative Living. Create your life of Self-Loving Fulfillment.

It is important to know what we want to believe and achieve, so that we can keep these life goals active; and bring us what we want, through SheEffectively™ being aware of, and productively regulating our own Thoughts and actions.

We can continue to create our own destiny, and SheChange™ our own reality, based on how we choose to continue to proactively ReShape™ WellBalance™ as a standard for our ongoing Thoughts, feelings and aspirations.

May you be Blessed to live Maatfully™ every day . .

247

Self-Worksheet 27:
On Making S.M.A.R.T. Goals

SMART goals help improve achievement and success. A SMART goal clarifies exactly what is expected and the measures used to determine if the goal is achieved and successfully completed.

A SMART goal is:

S = Specific: concrete, tangible steps and goals
Specific (and strategic): Linked to position summary, departmental goals/mission, and/or overall School of Medicine goals and strategic plans. Answers the question— "Who" and "What".

M = Measurable: how you'll know you've completed this goal, a tangible result. The success toward meeting the goal can be measured. Answers the question—"How"

A = Achievable: something you are capable of doing
Attainable/Achievable: Goals are realistic and can be achieved in a specific amount of time and are reasonable.

R = Realistic: something you can do given everything else in your life. Relevant and realistic: The goals are aligned with current tasks and projects and focus in one defined area; include the expected result.

T = Time-limited Frame
Time frame: Goals have a clearly defined time-frame including a target or deadline date.

EXAMPLES OF S.M.A.R.T. GOALS

These are <u>NOT</u> S.M.A.R.T. goals:

"Jada will improve her writing skills."
This does not identify a measurement or time frame, nor identify why the improvement is needed or how it will be used.

1. I want to be healthier.
2. I want to be a famous singer.
3. I will work in internet advertising.
4. I will own a house by next July.

These are S.M.A.R.T. goals:

We have identified a goal to improve communications with administrative staff by implementing a staff newsletter.

Jada will complete a business writing course by March, 2022 and will publish the first monthly newsletter by December 2022.

Jada will gather input and/or articles from others in the department and draft the newsletter for supervisor review, and when approved by her supervisor, distribute the newsletter to staff by the 30th of each month.

1. I will lose 30 lbs. by August 5, 2022.
2. I will work out for a minimum of 3 days a week by July, 2021.
3. I will create a first 5 goals of my business by February 24, 2022.
4. I will SheChange™ 3 Self-sabotaging habits by February 24, 2022.

SMART Goal Planning Form

Please write and number 3 S.M.A.R.T. Goals.

Specific – WHO? WHAT?

_____
_____
_____
_____

Measurement/ Assessment – HOW?

_____
_____
_____
_____
_____

Attainable/ Achievable – REASONABLE?

_____
_____
_____
_____
_____

Relevant/ Realistic – EXPECTED RESULT?

_____

_____

_____

_____

_____

_____

_____

_____

_____

_____

BY - Timed Limited Frame – WHEN?

_____

_____

_____

_____

_____

_____

✦ *Self-Worksheet 28:*
5 Simple Ways To Make Your Day More Peaceful . . .

"Be who you be, 'cause you can't be no one else . . ."
~ Lena Horne as quoted by Dionne Warwick

. . . Have you ever felt like you want to be more peaceful more regularly . . ?

And do you also feel like it would be nice to be so, but it would just take too MUCH time & effort for you to be peaceful day-to-day ? Well, here's a great solution for you . . . Being instantly peaceful also doesn't have to take a lot of effort nor know-how

Here's our recipe of 5 simple ways to instantly make your day more peaceful . . .

1. **Seek the wisdom of others.**
2. **Just say no to your awful attitude.**
3. **Lighten up & do something that makes your heart laugh.**
4. **Stop and sing a song that puts you back in good spirits.**
5. **Slow Down and listen to your heart.**

. . . .

1. Seek out the wisdom of others
Find, then make a list of, and regularly engage your awareness in a few astute quotes, articles or books which can quickly refocus your attention on Thoughts such as, "I know how to just let things happen", "reclaiming my peace of mind", or "I can turn off my relentless judging of my Self and others".

As we're sure you know ~ what we are suggesting here is to put into action, the well-known notions that "practice makes perfect" and that "kultivating™ a thing increases a thing" . . .

253

2. Just say "no" to an awful attitude

Here's a really simple and quick way to unseat an awful day, (usually caused by an equally awful attitude):

Instead of trying to prove your Self as right in a prolonged disagreement . . . simply shift from the emotional and verbal stance of inflexible embattlement to actually saying something like, "thank you, I see . . . (my own error; your point of view; what you meant, etc.), thanks, I'm good."

And, when someone else tries to "make peace" with, or [actually dares to] admit their own error to you ~ stop to actually listen, acknowledge and verbally accept a genuinely offered apology ~ rather than gloating or acting superior about it ~ as so many folk today are prone to do.

Both responses require a bit of Self-reflection, honesty, strength of character, courage and even a little humility, but they also promptly return you to your previously lost sense of inner-peace.

Now for those who honestly suffer from constantly apologizing for simply living your life, where it would be the case that saying "I'm sorry" would only reinforce already disproportionate feelings of inadequacy and separateness.

For you, we suggest the use of the response, "excuse me" instead. This way, you're being accountable for your actions while not putting your Self down by doing so. This is a more appropriate response, one which will actually allow you to feel better about your Self, as a benevolent result of your having done so.

So, if you really want to quickly return to a sense of peacefulness in a prolonged disagreement; the next time you hear a genuinely offered apology, simply pause to gracefully accept it. And when you come to realize that you've blundered or erred your Self, do "courage up" to quickly say so.

And so, the next time you feel unfairly criticized, simply pause to take a deep breath before you actually "act out" with over-reaction and then ask your Self if this might not be a good time to stay seated; or to ground your Self in quiet inner-peace-keeping, by sincerely offering an heart-felt "thank you for sharing your opinion."

254

3. Lighten up & do something that makes your heart laugh

Simple. Stop your negative thinking and feeling by simply indulging your Self in a moment of having a real sense of humor & authentic delight . . . like when you were still an unfettered and naturally carefree child . . . engage in something that delights your sense of innocence . . . something that genuinely makes you laugh at the very the core of your being . . .

4. Stop and sing a song that puts you back in your own good spirits

One of the simplest ways you can quickly reseat your Self in a peaceful, good spirited state again, is to either play (or sing if it works for you) one or more spirit-pleasing songs.

It allows you to shift your feelings easily, because your doing so instantly transports you from the depths of having angry, frustrated or stressful feelings ~ to heights of

your having calm, happy or delighted feelings (depending on the song(s) and on how much you delight in hearing or singing the song(s)). It's a naturally effective, yet simple form of "creative visualization".

I know you've heard of; "fake it until you make it" . . . well conversely, this is a case for you to proactively, "sing it until you uplift it" . . .

5. Slow down & simply listen to your heart

As you strive to live a more peaceful and "heartfelt" life; regularly pause to reconnect with the very pulse of your Being. When you can acknowledge (and put into action) that life doesn't have to be so non-stop, immediate or shallow to be meaningful for you, then you can begin to live a more peaceful life . . .

Simply said, peacefulness is gained by merely taking the time and making an effort to become more aware of something as subtle, yet essential, as your often ignored life-regulating heart pulse.

Here's a rather easy way to gain a deeper sense of your own place of inner-peace. Here's a way you can promptly bring about wholly potent benefits; including an increased awareness of your own natural inner-strength, resilience and ability to reconnect with, and enjoy the benefit of seating in your own authentic state of inner-peace.

And it's a really simple thing to do . . .

Just mindfully pause, right now. That's right, simply pause from reading this for a moment, to focus on, and be mindfully aware of the often ignored, vital reverberation of your own, very precious, and very under-acknowledged, heart beat . . .
can you feel it ? . . .

Listen, can you hear it?

. . . And as you are pausing now to do so . . . don't you . . . at the very least, start to feel a subtle shift in your awareness? . . .

A slight but deeper sense . . .

of your own Inner-Being . . .

Being? . . .

. . . SistahPeaceful™ Explorations . . .™

Journal about which of "The 5 Simple Ways" Resonate With You:

- *Seek the wisdom of others*
- *Just say no to your awful attitude*
- *Lighten up & do something that makes your heart laugh*
- *Stop and sing a song that puts you back in good spirits*
- *Slow Down and listen to your heart*
- *Unsure about which*
- *None of them did, could not relate*
- *None of them I have my own I prefer*

Journal about which of "The 5 Simple Ways" You Will Try:

- *Seek the wisdom of others*
- *Just say no to your awful attitude*
- *Lighten up & do something that makes your heart laugh*
- *Stop and sing a song that puts you back in good spirits*
- *Slow down and listen to your heart*
- *Unsure about which*
- *None of them, could not relate*
- *None of them I have my own I prefer*

PART 3

28 Weekly ReShapings™

*"Whatever you desire or require
is already planted on your pathway . . ."*
~ Florence Shovel Shinn

*ReShaping™ Week 1:*

Willingly ReShape™
Self-Negating Auto-Thoughts

"Act as though I Were, and I Am . . ."
~ Unknown

Detect your hidden Self-Negating Auto-Thoughts, which are now escaping your Awareness and instead, appear as your Negative Feelings.

Be Patient with your Negative Thoughts today, knowing that you have the Power of Choice.

Be willing to identify and ReShape™ any and all Negative Thoughts this week, knowing that they become your Feelings.

Be Thoughtful now, use rational, Non-judgmental Self-Scrutiny, which will reveal the Deeper Meaning behind the disturbing Negative Thoughts.

Seat your Self in Patient Stillness, as you Explore, Confront, and SheChange™ any Uncomfortable or Irrational Thoughts.

Create a "Thought-Action-Habit SheChange™" journal, where you will list and review those ongoing Negative Thoughts, Habits, [Re]Actions and Patterns which you're ready to identify, list, work on, replace, let go of, and that which you're willing to "put your mind on proactively doing . . !" each day of this week.

ReShaping™ Week 2:
Move Past Undeniably Irrational Feelings

"Learn to be quiet enough to hear the genuine within yourself so that you can hear it in others."
~ Marian Wright Edelman

Don't allow your under-regulated or over-regulated Emotions to rule you.

Remember that the Underlying Source of your Irrational Feelings, are your Negative Auto-Thoughts.

Be Willing to examine your current Values for Unrealistic, Non-productive and Life-Restrictive "Shoulds", "Ought-Tos" and "Musts".

Choose to proactively use a "growth mindset" to SheChange™ your brain in order to create new "Thought-Action Habits".

Adjust any Irrational Feelings that aren't supported by hard evidence now.

Pick one Meaningfully WellBalanced™ Action to Uplift your down-turned Mindset today.

 *ReShaping™ Week 3:*
Kultivate™ Integral Faultless MamaWitful™ Words

"Only by learning to live in harmony with your contradictions can you keep it all afloat."
~ Audre Lorde

Pause [take 5 minutes] to remember a time when you were successful at regulating Negative Auto-Thoughts, Feelings, Habits or Patterns this week.

Dare to work on SheChanging™ one unwanted Habit or Pattern this week.

We procrastinate because SheChange™ is often mentally [and habitually] seen as a "hard" thing for us to do – so just start and stop saying you can't – be more willing – acknowledge that Self-efficacy is, actually rewarding – as you dare to exercise your growing sense of Self-confidence.

Challenge your Negatively distorted Auto-Thoughts [like all or nothing thinking] create and make a list of proactive Thoughts and affirmations with which you can replace them. Then regularly use them.

Take extra time to practice having more gratitude, to help you to develop the ability of feeling more appreciative (which is the State of being Happy with the way your Life is) feeling safe, not wanting, not striving; feeling a greater sense of inner calm and safely connected to others.

Spend time positively by being around folks actively making positive life-style choices: Learn to do things that pick up your SheSpirits™. Learn how to work with impairments, by trusting that they will become proactive tools, which will in time, enable you to overcome any of these blocks to Personal Successes.

# *ReShaping™ Week 4:*

Undeniable Actions
Which Kultivate™ New Habits

> *"There's always something to suggest that*
> *you'll never be who you wanted to be.*
> *Your choice is to take it or keep on moving."*
> *~ Phylicia Rashad*

Remember that your Words create your Actions.

Since your Actions Speak Louder than your Words, remember to Strive to Act with WellBalanced™ Forethought.

Mindfully regulate your Auto-Thoughts today, Deliberately ReShaping™ wishful objectives [Words] into successful Actions.

Create motivational flashcards to help keep your newest Goals in the forefront of your proactive task-list. Write your "Pros of SheChanging™" on one side, and your "Losses of Staying the Same", on the other.

Refer to this list often this week.

Strive to be emotionally WellBalanced™ today.

Emotional regulation is the Key goal this week.

Practice developing your ability to learn how to tolerate, accept, work with and rise above any difficult emotions, negative feelings, which are the sources of those "Blue" moods.

ReShaping™ Week 5:

Purposefully Use Self-Affirmations™ Daily

"I Am WellBalanced™ and Well Adjusted in Mind, Spirit and Body; I Am Self-Affirmative™, Love-Centered and SistahPeaceful™."
~ *AfraShe Asungi*

Self-Affirmations™ are simply positive statements which can help you to challenge and remove Self-Sabotaging and Automatic Negative Thoughts [ANTs].

By repeating them frequently, you'll come to Believe them, then you'll Start to make Positive Life-Affirmative SheChanges™.

Look for ways to actuate the highest of Humin™ Virtues; Forgiveness, Aptitude, Perseverance, Courage, Justice, or Modesty.

Strive to further affirm a Character Style more akin to the qualities of fine jade; being Peaceful, Benevolent, Loyal, Virtuous, and Compassionate.

Self-Affirm and celebrate those days when your Knowing Purpose is Clear.

Dare to acknowledge your growing Womin-Affirmative™ Attitude!

SheAffirm™ your Unique WominBeing™ regularly by saying;

"I Am WellBalanced™, Well Adjusted in Mind, Spirit and Body; I Am Self-Affirmative™, Love-Centered and SistahPeaceful™".

ReShaping™ Week 6:
Conquer & Control Your Habits

"I have learned over the years that when one's mind is made up, this diminishes fear; knowing what must be done does away with fear."
~ Rosa Parks

Habits are merely the result of Thoughts, Feelings and Actions, repeated so often that, they become automatic and unconscious.

Clarify your Feelings; the more you can name them, the more you can manage them!

Be Mindful of your Under-regulated or Over-regulated Emotions; don't allow them to rule your Thoughts today.

Measuring the costs & benefits of resistance, say, "Yes it seems, hard but I can do hard things."

Check your level of Gratitude, so that it's not overwhelmed by (or maybe) it's actually (your) misread Ingratitude.

Sub it out when it's interfering with your success. There are people you can hire who are better able than you – learn when it's best to let them do "the work" for you, instead.

Remember that from time to time, our lives can be Stressful due to life's natural circumstances; attempt to recognize that some negative situations are just part of living and are not avoidable. We all have "bad days". Just endeavor to remember to be patient at those times; that better days will surely come again.

ReShaping™ Week 7:
Let Go of Irrefutably Self-Sabotaging Patterns

*"Embrace what makes you unique,
even if it makes others uncomfortable.
I didn't have to become perfect because I've learned throughout my journey that
perfection is the enemy of greatness."*
~ Janelle Monae

Refrain from any disparaging behavior you might be directing at your Self or others today.

When Negative Habits consistently undermine your Efforts, they are a form of psychological Self-harm.

Be willing to face your mistakes and weaknesses and replace them with help from others who are stronger in those areas.

The Roots of Self-Sabotage are found in Recurring Habits of Low Self-Esteem, and persistent Negative Thoughts and Emotions, which are continually Intensified by other Previous Failures.

Beat Self-Sabotage by Scrutinizing your Auto-Thoughts, Feelings, and Beliefs about your Self, especially when they cause you to Fail to Obtain your Goals.

Challenge negatively distorted Thoughts [such as all or nothing thinking], augmenting negatives and with a list of Proactive Thoughts and Affirmations, with which you can replace them.

Spend your Time Positively by being around others enacting positive life-style choices; learn to do things that pick up your SheSpirits™.

ReShaping™ Week 8:
Mutually Respectful
& Emotionally Fluid Relationships™

We have to talk about liberating minds as well as liberating society.
- Angela Davis

Are you taking anything too Personally Right Now?

Be Especially Patient with your Self and Others today.

Meaningful Relationships don't simply happen. Make Time to Engage in Mutually Respectful and Fluid Relationship with others.

Take time to Realize and Appreciate the Subtle Truth Behind the present Confusion.

"A meaningful relationship is one where you can feel free to be your authentic Self." You feel "connected, accepted, wanted and cherished", and you help your partner feel the same way.

Outwit Irrational Intolerance by Seating your Self in Patient Stillness.

Look for ways to be appreciative of and emphasize any Mutual Relationship Objectives this week!

ReShaping™ Week 9:

Challenge Troublesome ANTs [Automatic Negative Thoughts]

"An unrestrained Spirit and Insightful Self-Clarity™ are the rewards of successfully controlling your senses . . ."
~ Afrikan Wisdom

Build the Resilience to Patiently Challenge your ANTs [Automatic Negative Thoughts] by replacing them with More Reassuring and Self-Affirmational Thoughts. According to their creator, Dr. A. Beck, a few ANTS are:

- o *Black and White Thinking [Using words like "always," "never," and "every"].*
- o *Focusing on the Negative [dismissing the good and focusing only on the negative]*
- o *Fortune Telling [thinking the worst is the only outcome].*
- o *Being Ruled by "Shoulds", etc.*
- o *Mind Reading [that you know another's Thoughts absolutely].*
- o *Taking Things Personally.*
- o *Say, "I'm Thoughtfully choosing to feel calm and peaceful now."*

Replace your ANTs with Affirmational Thoughts, for they help you to SheChange™ the Negative or Fear-based beliefs, they serve as a distraction.

As you focus on the affirmation, it keeps any ANTs or other racing Thoughts at bay.

ReShaping™ Week 10:
Promote A Refined Attitude

*"The greatest discovery of all times is
that a person can change her future
by merely changing her attitude."*
~ Oprah Winfrey

You are Absolutely Remarkable!

Be Patient with your Self and Others this week.

Be Willing to investigate your Core Beliefs, so they no longer stall, nor sabotage your Life.

Strive to do one Act of Random Kindness today.

Strive to identify your "buts" and regularly replace them with "ands" instead.

Analyze your anxiety-based Core Beliefs for "Benefits and Costs".

Review, whether the Costs outweigh the Benefits, then spend some time considering if it's time to let this particular Belief go.

Strive to Make Better Choices as a Way to make life Better.

ReShaping™ Week 11:
Self-Affirmatively Identify
& Replace
Cognitive Distortions

"Hope and fear cannot occupy the same space at the same time. Invite one to stay."
~ Maya Angelou

Strive to clarify your feelings, the more you can Name them, the more you can Manage them.

Challenge Negatively Distorted Thoughts [like All or Nothing Thinking] Noticing the Negative Ones and having a list of Proactive Thoughts that you can replace them with.

SheAffirmatively™ ask your Self: Is this Thought true?

Does having this Thought serve me?

Is there another explanation or another way of looking at things?

What advice would I give someone else who had this Thought?

Spend time positively by being around positive life-styles choices: learn to do things that pick up your SheSpirits™.

SheCreate™ a more well directed, Womin-Affirmative™ Attitude.

Smile . . .

ReShaping™ Week 12:

SheCreate™ A Proactive
& Realizable SheDestiny™

"You may not always have a comfortable life and you will not always be able to solve all of the world's problems at once; but don't ever underestimate the importance you can have, because history has shown us that courage can be contagious, and hope can take on a life of its own."
~ Michelle Obama

Be Grateful and Graceful with the Gifts you have been Granted.

Look for new Actions, which Enhance or Expand your Life Goals.

Be an Actionable Womin™, Proactively ReShaping™ Her own Life-Affirmative SheDestiny™

Pause to Ensure that whatever you do in the Name of Love, always includes Being Kind.

Act in Accordance with the ageless Doctrine that "your Thoughts Really Do Determine your SheDestiny™".

Create and follow one SMART goal to redirect Positive Actions and help you to Know when to say no.

Small doable habits really keep you Proactively moving towards long lasting SheChange™, little by little, until you Gain the Win.

ReShaping™ Week 13:

SheAffirm™
Your Own Dance Regularly

"We can say 'Peace on Earth'.
We can sing about it, preach about it or pray about it,
but if we have not internalized the mythology to make it happen inside us,
then it will not be."
- Betty Shabazz

Appreciate All that has Transpired so far to make you . . . YOU !

You are Worthy of Love and Respect. Always.

Be Mindful of your Self-Judgment and Self-Criticism this week.

Create or review a Daily Self-Affirmation™ Plan. Add any meaningful positive Thoughts and Actions, which SheAffirms™ your authentically Unique Womin-Being™.

Best Self-Critical Misjudgment by Seating your Self in Patient Stillness, positive Thoughts and uplifting Self-Affirmations™.

Honor SheCreative™ Spontaneity this week! Be Artfully Fluid!

Add positive reminders; post notes, SheInspirational™ quotes and other Womin-Affirmative™ reminders.

Take 5 minutes to Dance Jubilantly with Your Self each day of this week (with your barefeet touching the earth, if possible).

285

ReShaping™ Week 14:

Find "Evidence of Truth"
For Any Imbalanced Thoughts

"When you take care of yourself, you're a better person for others. When you feel good about yourself, you treat others better."
~ Solange Knowles

Practice using Self-help tools to overturn your Self-Doubts, by asking Smart Questions, which lead you to Challenge your own Negative Assumptions and find more appropriate answers than you initially believed were needed.

Don't Believe your Self-Doubting Thoughts without Evidence of them actually being Reality-Based.

Address undeveloped Executive Functioning by identifying Thoughts which Improve Positive Outcomes and Enhance your Quality of Life opportunities.

Take time to acknowledge any Negative Emotions which led to your negative behavior, or were caused by Irrational Thoughts.

Consider the evidence for or against those Negating Thoughts.

Notice what you say to your Self when you engage in Self-sabotaging behavior. Take time to observe and write down all of your Negative Self-Talk, however Silly or Unrealistic it may seem.

Refute any Negative Self-Talk with Self-Supportive Affirmations.

ReShaping™ Week 15

Mistress™ Any Irrational Fears & Self-Criticisms

"When I liberate myself, I liberate others. If you don't speak out ain't nobody going to speak out for you."
~ Fannie Lou Hamer

Irrational Fears are the Groundwork of Panic & Anxiety.

Scan your recent Thoughts for undue Self-Criticism & unreasonable Harshness.

… and Dare to Practice Accepting your Self.

Outmaneuver Misadventure as you Seat your Self in Patient Stillness.

Look to and Use your Self-Affirmative Sources Now !

Be generous while Remembering that for Generosity to work in Favor of your WellBalance™, it can't be Self-Effacing.

So, when being Authentically Generous, be Authentically Aware of your own needs.

Be Open to that which appears to Threaten your Proactive Core Beliefs.

Actively Engage in the Elevated Arts of Practicing Self-Acceptance and Self-Appreciation.

ReShaping™ Week 16

Identify and Proactively ReShape™
Self-Sabotaging Thinking

"Those that don't got it, can't show it.
Those that got it, can't hide it."
~ Zora Neale Hurston

Practice using the "ABCDE Rational Psychology" Model to SheChange™ & SheCreate™ a more fruitfully WellBalanced™ Life.

Remember to Be Patient with your Self today, by doing this:

- *Activating Situation: Your Lover calls it quits suddenly.*
- *Beliefs: "I can't live my life without them".*
- *Consequence: Negative Feelings & Actions:*
  Negative Feelings: Anxious Thoughts, Anger, Depression.
  Negative Actions: Stalking an Ex-Lover, not able to eat, missing work.
- *Dispute Irrational Thoughts: "They were often unavailable".*

- *Effect of using More Rational Challenging: Able to calm down, use supportive resource, start dating again, take time to do more Self-Work. "I'm attractive and can find a new lover".*

Remember to Seat your Self in Patient Stillness each day.

Implement a daily ReShaping™ plan to better manage additional fear-driven stress and anxiety symptoms!

ReShaping™ Week 17:

Be Wisely Guided by SheAffirmative™ MamaWit™

*"I am no longer accepting the things I cannot change.
I am changing the things I cannot accept."
~ Angela Davis*

Be Benevolent as you reconnect with your Highest Wisdom today.

Note the Pros and Cons concerning the current Issues and Dilemmas.

Kultivate™ a Strategic Plan for a more Harmonious Outcome.

Get more exercise, to restore your attention levels – take short breaks.

Center on Happiness. Be Willing to limit technology and proactively do those things which make your Heart Smile.

Learn to be more flexible and open with your thinking solutions.

Use slow breathing to center and calm your Attitude.

Find more "Do-able" choices as regular problem-solving tools.

Practice Emotionally Regulating your Fears by using a Strengths-based and "Positive-Self-talk" approach today.

Be receptive and amenable to differing opinions.

ReShaping™ Week 18:

Unimpeachable Self-Appreciation, Self-Regard & Self-Respect

"A woman's gifts will make room for her."
~ Hattie McDaniel

Don't let any misguided Auto-Thoughts provoke Negative Feelings.

Maintain respectful Self-Regard, while Preserving or Restoring [WellBalanced™] Emotions, which uphold Self-Dignity and Gratitude.

Identify any Thoughts which are creating Fear-Based Feelings of Stress, and other Negative Self-Defeating Emotions.

Consider healthier Self-Appreciative alternatives now.

Ask for ShePositive™ support from others.

Be easygoing and carefree with your Self and others today.

Love and encourage the Womin™ that you Know you are Becoming.

Ask for Awakened ShePositiveness™ . . . Look for signs which will divulge the Subtle Truth behind the Present Confusion.

Journal, do ShePositive™ things and Look to your Dreams for Guidance Now !

ReShaping™ Week 19:

Manage Disharmonious [Angry] Feelings Or Emotions

"Just don't give up on what you're trying to do.
Where there is love and inspiration,
I don't think you can go wrong."
~ Ella Fitzgerald

Be Patient and Kind with your Self and others today.

Mindsets are merely learned (approving or disapproving) evaluative Thoughts and preferences towards certain things (people, places, or situations); therefore, they can be SheChanged™.

Consciously Kultivate™ SheAffirmative™ Thoughts which are supportive of Greater WellBalance™ and Happiness this week.

Appreciate what's working in your life now and proactively celebrate what's really working for you right now.

Notice the compliments you receive this week.

Spend more time building on your strengths rather than your weaknesses – in order to get successful outcomes more often.

If time-blindness is an issue, use daily calendars where you use them along with goal-setting tools for effective future planning. Learn how much time it takes to do something (a task).

Then Mindfully engage in "do-able" time-limited tasks.

Regularly practice the perception that, "life is not measured by the number of breaths we take, but by the moments that take our breaths away."

ReShaping™ Week 20:

Realize & Appreciate Your Inherent Self-Worth

*"The path to healing means going beyond the boundaries you are used to. We can find gratitude for where we are, because that helps us to identify what we want or where we've come from.
But beyond what we think are our limits is so much more than we can even imagine."*
~ Alicia Keys

Be patient with your Self and others today.

Ask for the MamaWit™ Wisdom to Know the utmost value of Kultivating™ inherent Self-Worth.

Know and Honor that inherent Self-Worth comes from inside your Self and your unmistaken understanding that you are Unique, Valuable, and Worthy.

Venture to separate Authentic Expectations of your Self from the Beliefs and Expectations of others.

Make a New Habit of consciously stopping the overflow of Negative Self-talk.

Take the time to enjoy the Joy of Being in the present by Mindfully focusing on what you are doing at lease 15 minutes every day.

Kultivate™ being your own best friend.

Strive to Flourish . . .

. . . then rise to the task of being authentically you !

ReShaping™ Week 21:

Be Still . . .
& Kultivate™ Valid,
Harmonious Thoughts™

"Don't settle for average.
Bring your best to the moment.
Then, whether it fails or succeeds, at least you know
you gave all you had.
We need to live the best that's in us."
~ Angela Bassett

Don't confuse fleeting Feelings with valid Thoughts.

Feelings are seldom fact-based.

Feelings are just emotional Thoughts.

Pause to appreciate the beauty of simple things.

Take care of your emotional needs on the regular.

Refrain from making Self-disparaging commentaries . . .

Acknowledge to your Self regularly that, you deserve respectful treatment.

Embrace the unique Womin-Being™ you are and fully express the unique energy that is the very core of your Womin-Being™.

This is Authentic Self-Love . . . and while it is not an easy thing to do, you come to appreciate the out-comes it brings.

Be Still and simply listen now.

ReShaping™ Week 22:
Forgive Your Self Regularly

"If you prioritize yourself, you are going to save yourself."
~ Gabrielle Union

Bring forth a higher love today,

Dare to stand midway between it ALL.

Allow your Self room to make mistakes, observing mistakes as a Path to attaining new knowledge.

Be patient and kind with your Self-Advancement goals.

Your WellBalanced™ mental health depends on your ability to reduce and let go of fear, hurt and anger, especially at your Self.

Acknowledge and SheAffirm™ your body as a user-friendly environment.

Stop comparing your Self to others, stop unduly worrying about others' opinions.

Refrain from placing your Worth in how your body looks.

Process your Fears, and then dare to move beyond them. Don't be afraid to let go of toxic Thoughts, people and situations.

Learn how to . . .

and then Trust your Self to make good decisions for your Self.

ReShaping™ Week 23:

Kultivate™ Non-Judgmental Awareness

*"It is so liberating to really know what I want,
what truly makes me happy, what I will not tolerate.
I have learned that it is no one else's job
to take care of me but me."*
~ Beyonce' Knowles

Regularly engage in WellBalanced™ Thoughts of Loving-Kindness with Your Self and others.

Don't despair.

Even when you fail or make a misstep, simply reset your Self upright and on your Desired Path again.

Let Non-judgmental awareness sweep away any vestiges of Self-Dejection.

Strive to nurture your Self in the warm embrace of elevated Self-compassion, use sympathetic rather than judgmental dialog today.

Consistently make time to exercise and enjoy being Kinder, and accepting of Self and others, especially those who present you with overly-defensive resistance!

Exercise Non-judgmental awareness now, by simply repeating 3 times, "I Love and Accept my Self exactly as I am . . . I Love and Accept others exactly as they are . . ."

ReShaping™ Week 24:

Promote Intentional Self-Kindness & Self-Appreciation

"I have the nerve to walk my own way, however hard, in my search for reality, rather than climb upon the rattling wagon of wishful illusions."
~ Zora Neale Hurston

Stop . . .

Being Hard on your Self . . .

Refrain from punishing your Self for your mistakes.

Instead, kindly accept that you too, are imperfectly perfect, then strive to be patient and gentle with your Self in the face of any ([real or perceived) failed challenges.

Intentionally equalize Self-Compassion with Thoughts of Self-approval.

Know the difference between telling your Self that you're "not good enough" and reminding your Self that you intend to "work to make things better".

Practice Loving-Kindness and Self-Forgiveness regularly.

Stop punishing your Self for your mistakes.

Employ a growth mindset, viewing challenges as opportunities to grow.

Be mindful.

Employ compassion and generosity towards your Self this week.

ReShaping™ Week 25:

Gently Yoke
& Forgive Your Inner-Critic

"I'm convinced that we Black women possess a special indestructible strength that allows us to not only get down, but to get up, to get through, and to get over."
~ Janet Jackson

Your inner-critic is merely an integrated pattern of Negative, destructive Thoughts, often aimed at our Selves or toward others.

Generating unkind, unwarranted Feelings of shame is your inner-critic's specialty.

Similar to fear, its original role was to Prohibit us from veering too far from unforgiving social rules.

Unharnessed, it's just another unmonitored inner voice which Over-judges, Over-criticizes, or Over-demeans us, even when such Self-criticism does not accurately justify our doing so.

An unregulated, and overly active inner-critic often takes toll on your emotional Well-Being and healthy Self-esteem.

Stop ruminating; it will only make you Feel worse and it won't solve the problem at hand.

Convert any overly pessimistic Thoughts into more rational and realistic Affirmations.

Let Self-compassion and Loving Kindness be your grounding Guides!

ReShaping™ Week 26:

Mindfully Detach
from Your Anxious Thoughts

"Whenever I feel bad, I use that feeling to motivate me to work harder. I only allow myself one day to feel sorry for myself.
I ask myself, 'What are you gonna do about it?' I use the negativity to fuel the transformation into a better me."
~ Beyoncé Knowles

Willingly ReShape™ your anxious Thoughts today.

Be Willing to immerse in proactive Thoughts, which are neither Self-critical, nor overly Self-Negative, and Actively ReShape™ your Thoughts.

Be more affirmative about what you've done, and what you perceive you are capable of doing, or even how you think about who you are.

Celebrate your Successes, even the small ones. Spend 5 minutes daily writing about those things which made you feel good the previous day . . .

Make a list of at least six Self-Affirming words or phrases and regularly use them.

Practice Gratitude. Name three things you're Grateful for today.

Take a moment at least three times each day of this week, to pause to ask your Self if you're Thinking Positively; which will gently guide you to remember to focus on building a more unyieldingly Positive Attitude.

Occasionally Check-in with your Self, detaching from any anxiety-driven Thoughts this week . . .

ReShaping™ Week 27:

Be A Womin™
Of Impeccable Character

"You don't make progress by standing on the sidelines, whimpering and complaining. You make progress by implementing ideas."
~ Shirley Chisholm

Humility, Graciousness, Patience and Compassion are the presiding Emotional Tones of the week.

Remember that Words have Power.

Say only what you mean, using your Words for the Purpose of Harmony, Truth and Goodwill each day.

Be Impeccable with your Thoughts, Feelings and Words: practice speaking with Thoughtful Integrity.

Avoid speaking against your Self or Engaging in Gossip about others this week.

Venture to graciously reply, "Thank you", when others positively compliment you, and dare to genuinely mean it.

Be a Womin™ of Impeccable Character this week!

ReShaping™ Week 28:

Acknowledge & Honor Your AnSistahral™ Guides & SheGuardians™

"I have Armaments you do not Know of,
I have Ways which will Astound you . . ."
~ Unknown

Regularly . . .

Acknowledge, Salute and Honor Those "Who Open Doors" . . .

Dare to Ask Them to Guide you to Know Their Great SheMysteries™, which we've come to honor as our own Unique SheDestinies™.

Call on the Great Ones to Bring you Endless Joy, as you Dare to Walk your own Unique Life's Path.

Ask for Their Unique Kasmik™ SheInspiration™ to Teach you to Come to Know when your own Thoughts are Neither Clear nor Wise.

Kindly Entreat Them to Be, and to Actuate your Highest Kasmikally™ Aligned Sense of Authentic Self-Knowing.

Then . . .

Dare to Perceive, Believe and Achieve your own Unique Great SheDestiny™ . . !

Then . . .

Venture to Be your own Greatest Life's Design . . !

Then . . .

Then . . .

. . .OFFER DEEP GRATITUDE TO OUR MAATFULLY™ GUIDING

& PROTECTIVE ANSISTAHS™ . . .

An Afterword:

Where To Go From Here?

elieve in Your Self . . .
While Kultivating™ Loving Kindness . . .

There's two other things I'd like to suggest here, one is for those Wimmin™ who're using this Self-Workbook on their own:

First, after reading through this Self-Workbook at least once; please continue to freely use any part of this Self-Workbook, its Self-Worksheets, or any of its other resources on a "as needed" basis.

The second is for Wimmin™ who are working with a therapist:

Discuss just how they recommend that you use the materials found in this Self-Workbook.

Either way, review the general questions and Self-Worksheets which you've found useful. Don't hesitate to revisit any chapters which you find helpful.

Review the Following Questions:

Three positive things I now know about my Self are:

_____

_____

_____

_____

List and SheChange™ old habits – create new habits

_____

_____

When I am scared or fearful I can:

_____

_____

When I am ruminating

_____

_____

Three tools I can now use to WellBalance™ my Thoughts, Feelings, and Actions are:

_____

_____

My top 5 affirmations:

_____

_____

_____

_____

_____

My daily ReShaping™ routine is now:

_____

_____

_____

_____

Realize that you can SheChange™ almost anything. Give any new habits lots of energy through practicing them or imagining your Self doing them. Work on only one or two habits at a time that requires Self-control.

Continue to proactively venture to recognize, gradually find, and effectively SheChange™ your Thoughts, Feelings, and Habits enough that over time you learn to regularly Kultivate™ a more fulfilling and loving sense of Self.

Continue to become a more purposeful Mistress™, She Who "weaves generous and wondrous SheChange™ into your life ", and dares to regularly ReShape™ old fears and Negativity into your own Self-Affirmative SheDestiny™!

A SPECIAL NOTE TO MY READERS:

 s I'm busy writing and editing this ReShaping™ Self Workbook, the Biden - Harris Administration have just declared and signed Juneteenth as our 2nd Afrikan American National Federal Holiday !!!!!

And to paraphrase here, ". . . 'cause I Know that my AnSistahs™ got my back . . . ™ "

So . . . Happy 1st Juneteenth (June 19th, 2021) as our 2nd National Federal Holiday to y'all Sistahs in the 'Root !!!!!!!!!!

   *KaraShebaa Ma™ . . . !*

May you be Blessed to live Maatfully™ every day . . .

OUR RESOURCES & REFERENCES

Beck, A.T. 1976. Cognitive Therapy and the Emotional Disorders. International Universities Press. New York.

Boyles, A. 2015. The Anxiety Toolkit. A Perigee Book. New York.

Carnegie, D. 2004. How To Stop Worrying and Start Living. Pocket Books, New York.

Ellis, A., and Harper, R. 1961. A Guide to Rational Living.: Wilshire Books. North Hollywood.

Gillihan, S. J. 2016. Retrain Your Brain. Althea Press. Berkeley.

Hay, L. H. 2016. Mirror Work: 21 Days to Heal Your Life.

Hay House. California.

Hay, L. H. 1984. Heal Your Body: The Mental Causes for Physical Illness and the Metaphysical Way to Overcome Them. Hay House. California.

https://www.psychologytoday.com/basics/habit-formation

Kabat-Zinn, J. 1990. Full Catastrophe Living. Delta. New York.

McKay, M. and Fanning, P. 1992. 2nd ed. Self-Esteem. New Harbinger. Oakland.

Oluwole, S. B., 1984. "The Rational Basis of Yoruba Ethical Thinking," The Nigerian Journal of Philosophy, 4 (1&2): 14–25.

Toller, L. 2007. My Mother's Rules: A Practical Guide to Becoming an Emotional Genius. Agate Imprint. Chicago.

Toller, L. 2012. Making Marriage Work: New Rules for an Old Institution. Agate Imprint. Chicago.

OUR MUSIK LIST RECOMMENDATIONS

Beyoncé - "Spirit" + "Bigger" Extended cut (Official Video)

https://www.youtube.com/watch?v=hiqLtqMDrXQ

Alicia Keys - A Woman's Worth (Official HD Video)

https://www.youtube.com/watch?v=JtMUIwOE2ss

India.Arie - Just Do You

https://www.youtube.com/watch?v=qXpaJMg3q8I

Alice Coltrane -A Love Supreme

https://www.youtube.com/watch?v=89c00fGC838

Dianne Reeves- Limbo

https://www.youtube.com/watch?v=S_UWnSMuzzA

Dianne Reeves -Ancient Source

https://www.youtube.com/watch?v=Pe8AyXEOlqY

Whitney Houston, Mariah Carey - When You Believe (Official HD Video)

https://www.youtube.com/watch?v=LKaXY4IdZ40

To Be Young, Gifted and Black (Live at Philharmonic Hall, New York, NY - October 1969)

https://www.youtube.com/watch?v=tq6b--vIcF8

Candance Glover When You Believe

https://www.youtube.com/watch?v=2AMiGXyFp4s

Stephanie Mills - Home

https://www.youtube.com/watch?v=cnKQN7TF4hQ

Gladys Knight - I Hope You Dance

https://www.youtube.com/watch?v=gM_UJbTMY0M

Patti LaBelle - New Attitude (Official Music Video)

https://www.youtube.com/watch?v=QWfZ5SZZ4xE

Dionne Warwick Anyone Who Had A Heart 1964 Original Top 10 Hit

https://www.youtube.com/watch?v=qMsiGMKHJ8k

Minnie Riperton- Inside My Love

https://www.youtube.com/watch?v=UVniMFJYY1o

Deniece Williams - Free (Audio)

https://www.youtube.com/watch?v=OlLrn6AVV2s

Jean Carn - Revelation

https://www.youtube.com/watch?v=i8BS5xfzKmU&list=PLtUP-SvVKpi-dP0joXJPn8lSMZTDjssy9&index=1

Jean Carn - Naima (John Coltrane)

https://www.youtube.com/watch?v=yWTtZ015Z70&list=PLtUP-SvVKpi-dP0joXJPn8lSMZTDjssy9&index=7

Aretha Franklin - Ac-Cent-Tchu-Ate the Positive

https://www.youtube.com/watch?v=LDXnqmgtp7s

Aretha Franklin - Respect [1967] (Aretha's Original Version)

https://www.youtube.com/watch?v=6FOUqQt3Kg0

Tina Turner - Lotus Sutra _ Purity of Mind (2H Meditation)

https://www.youtube.com/watch?v=hYVbcoUdmlo

About The Author

www.AfraSheAsungi.com

AfraShe Asungi, HHHAS, MFA, MSW, LCSW, ReShaper™

*". . . Creating that which we call Fine Art is my Path
of Knowing, Being and Doing, Maat . . .
as I strive to "pull back the Veil" . . . Always . .
My Foundational Guiding SheCreative™
AfraMama™ Spiritual Principle is MAAT!"*

*~ AfraShe Asungi, HHHAS, MFA, LCSW,
SP WellBalance™ ReShaper™*

*Noted as being one of the "Founding Contributors" and "Grandmother" of the Modern
Goddess & Women's Spirituality Movement, AfraShe Asungi, HHHAS has been a*

published and exhibiting Social Justice & Gender Activist, Visionary, Visual Artist and an ordained Wimmin's™ Spiritual Shedoms™ & Inner-SheMystae™ Teacher for over 4 decades.

AfraShe is an independent researcher, publisher, practitioner and founding Tepaat Philasapher™, SheScribe™ and Instructress of the Afrakan® ® Philasophies™ and MaataSciences™ and MatriNubian™ PsychaSymbology™ and practices since early 70s.

As a visionary social justice and gender social activist artist, her work has been published, featured and her distinctive contributions have been acknowledged globally . . .

During the late 1970's visionary artist, AfraShe Asungi inaugurated a body of visual images & written philosophies, including a first of its kind collection entitled, "the Goddess Series . . . I ™" - to publicly "honor and affirm Black Wimmin™, Our Kultural™ uniqueness, and Herstorical Self-determination "as a positive norm."

The series was part of a larger body of paintings and writings, entitled "Amazons" and is significant for its mythic restructuring, delineation & depiction of "Strong, Self-Contained" & Self-governing Afrikan Goddess during the late 1970s & 1980s. Works

from this series continue to be featured in international publications and media.

In the early 80s and 90s, AfraShe envisioned and founded the landmark MAMAROOTS® AfraKamaatik® SpiraKultural™ Sistahood (1982), along with the publication, MAMAROOTS Triune Forum™ (1990) based on these landmark MatriNubian™ social /spiritual constructs which are Rooted in Our AfraKamaatik® Principles of Kasmik™ Harmony & Order.

AfraShe Asungi earned her Bachelor's degree in Fine Arts from Wayne State University. Her first Master's degree (MFA) in Fine Arts is in printmaking & Africana/ Asian/ Oceanic studies from the University of Chicago.

Currently, AfraShe lives in Long Beach, California, where as a psychotherapist and life coach in private practice, she encourages creative community wellness by offering personal and Spiritual growth services . . . and [of course] continues to "Live Maatfully™ and do the work . . ."

So, let me share a bit about my Self . . .

I'm a [rather unconventional] Psychospiritual, Solution-Focused and SpiraKulturally™-based psychotherapist (Licensed Clinical Social Worker); Certified WellBalance™ ReShaper™; Certified Life Purpose, Transitions & Wimmin's™ SpiraKultural™ Coach; Certified Substance Abuse & Relapse Counselor; Visionary Fine Artist; Intuitive Empath, and Gender Arts Activist.

> *You deserve and can have
> balance, success, satisfaction
> and authentic happiness
> in your life . . .
> and I'm here to help you . . .*

I'm a down-to earth, easy to talk to, Solution Focused, Womin-Affirmative™, and results-oriented counselor and coach, with the experience and the ability to effectively help you and your loved ones to successfully reach your specific life-change goals, which will also bring balance and a restored sense of satisfaction and peace of mind back into your lives.

Taking a common-sense approach, I use a unique combination of psychotherapy methods proven to be effective in helping you to resolve worrisome dramas, Self-sabotaging Thoughts and Emotions which have you stuck and held hostage in your personal and professional life; your romantic relationship; your marriage, partnership, family or academic problems.

You don't have to stay stuck in unsatisfactory relationships; feelings of isolation, anxiety, depression, a prolonged lack of Self-esteem.

~ This Self-Workbook can help you to Proactively ReShape™ your Self . . .

Typical results may include:

> ➤*a restored sense of hope and peace of mind;*
> ➤*happier and more satisfying relationships;*
> ➤*finally overcoming and moving beyond the blahs, blues and emotional misery;*
> ➤*moving beyond Self-sabotaging Thoughts, Emotions & Behaviors;*
> ➤*learning to have a happier, more fulfilling, SistahPeaceful™ life/ lifestyle . . .*

https://yhst-172736973-1.stores.yahoo.net/on-reshaping-wellbalanced-thoughts-poster.html

For info on AfraShe's "story", other books, artwork, and current projects visit her online at:

http://www.AfraSheAsungi.com

http://www.SheKulturalStudios.com

http://www.Aparthamaat.com

http://www.facebook.com/The.Goddess.Series.I?sk=wall

http://www.MAMAROOTSweb.org

AfraShe promotes creative community wellness as a psychotherapist in private practice.

You can learn more about these personal growth approaches at SistahPeace™ ReShaping™ WellBalance™ Counseling & Coaching Services :
http://www.SistahPeace.com

May you be Blessed to live Maatfully™ every day . . .

Thanks For Your Purchase:

As a special "Thank You"
for your interest
and purchase of this Maatful™ SheChange™ product,
we'd like to give you a gift
of a one-time 15% off one of Our products:

From Our "Maatfully ™ WellBalanced™ For Life Series",
Or
From Our "SheInspired™ For Life Press Series".
Or
From Our Other SheKultural™ Products:
https://yhst-172736973-1.stores.yahoo.net/on-reshaping-wellbalanced-thoughts-poster.html

If you found the contents from this Self-Workbook helpful or useful, we'd appreciate
your taking a few quick minutes to write a review or join our mailing list for updates
about our other books and works of art.
We'll be adding more books to Our Amazon Page,
so please check back for Our new updates . . .

May you be Blessed to live Maatfully™ every day . . .

Made in the USA
Middletown, DE
14 March 2022

62450784R10201